The Anxious Truth

By Drew Linsalata

The Anxious Truth

ISBN: 978-1-7346164-4-6

Cover design by Drew Linsalata

Edited by Hilary Jastram

 BOOKMARK

The Anxious Truth

Praise for *The Author*

"I have spent endless amounts on therapy, books, self-help booklets for my OCD, your story, Claire weeks, and your podcasts have been the only thing that's has helped me, truly grateful, I don't get too involved by commenting on podcasts, but I follow all your wonderful advice. Thanks Drew, you have helped me so much."

- Michele (Facebook comment, May 2020)

"Life-changing. This podcast is my go-to for anything anxiety!!! It truly has changed the way I deal with my anxiety disorder. Thank you Drew for providing this fantastic podcast! I've learned sooooo much."

- Stacy (Podcast review, May 2020)

"Get your life back. I found this podcast when I was desperately looking to understand what was going on in my life after experiencing panic and anxiety disorder. When I was at my worst, these podcasts helped me get through the day. The very detailed explanations about what was happening and how to recover from it were life-altering for me. I have been to multiple therapists who never touched the surface of what recovery looks like for those with these disorders. Thanks to Drew, this Podcast and the Facebook group, I'm thrilled to share that I am well on my way towards reaching 100% recovered medication-free."

- Monica (Podcast review, April 2020)

"No Nonsense Approach. I have listened to a lot of anxiety podcasts, been in anxiety Facebook groups, used Google and YouTube seeking answers throughout my anxiety journey. It wasn't until I found Drew, his podcast, and Facebook group that I started seeing real progress in my recovery from Generalized Anxiety Disorder. If you want to recover from anxiety/panic disorder, then look no further. This is the podcast for you and Drew also has a Facebook group with the same name 'The Anxious Truth'."

- Nicole (Podcast review, November 2019)

"I got my first paycheck today!! Which means I've been at my new job for 2 weeks now! Haven't been late, haven't had to leave, haven't called in sick (even though I almost did last week due to anxiety). Super-duper proud of myself. I could cry .Thank you so much Drew Linsalata I never thought I would be able to work again but here I am doing it."

- Suzzy (Facebook post, October 2019)

"I just wanted to say thank you so much to this group for giving me advice supporting me, thank you for Drew Linsalata on his amazing knowledge on anxiety and how to deal with it day-to-day.

I can say I never really understood my anxiety so I never really knew how to help myself now that I listen to podcasts I read everything I understand anxiety and my anxiety and my symptoms to a deeper level this group can do wonders Yes I may still have off days but that's okay it's a part of growing and learning.

I am determined to learn how to keep living with anxiety and understanding my triggers and letting them float over me!!"

- Tiah (Facebook post July 2019)

"I'd like to take a second to thank Drew Linsalata for helping me and many other people in this group. I didn't find The Anxious Truth until about 5 months ago when I was deeply paralyzed by my panic for 2 years prior, and sporadically throughout my life. I stumbled upon Drew's channel randomly on YouTube. It was like night and day. So many other videos for anxiety management ... they rely on feelings of comfort and positive mindsets, as well as snapping yourself out of it with distractions, or just taking medication till you are magically better...

The Anxious Truth is truly the best thing I've ever heard, and it has helped me so much to this day. This is the only way to recover and Drew knows what he is doing for sure!"
- Parker (Facebook post, August 2019)

"I love you!!!! I'm a panic disorder sufferer going on 7 years. You have been more helpful to me than anything. It is a daily battle to leave my house, but you calm my nerves and make me feel ok. Thank you."
- Lindsey (Instagram message, February 2020)

"THANK YOU! I am almost one month un-medicated after 4 years of being medicated. Your thoughts and teaching on anxiety are so so helpful! Thank you for being vulnerable and sacrificial in sharing for others!"

- Candace (Instagram message, October 2019)

"Really pay attention to Drew's podcasts and what he talks about doing. Make the hard decisions to overcome. 11 months ago I thought I was in a place I would never go out of. A few months ago I had my first moment of clarity when things started clicking and I could feel it working. One good day turned into two and then strings of good days. Anxiety wasn't trying to kill me, it was trying to warn me. And when I started accepting it, acknowledging it and then moving past...I felt like, well I can't even describe the plain and simple joy of it. I am so thankful for finding this group and Drew Linsalata. Just keep it up and I hope we can all talk to each one day about how much anxiety USED to be a problem for us."

- Mike (Facebook post, November 2018)

Resources

The Anxious Truth Website

https://theanxioustruth.com

The Anxious Truth Podcast and Social Links

https://theanxioustruth.com/links

Vital Recovery Skills – Breathing, Medication, Focus, and Relaxation

https://theanxioustruth.com/skills

An Anxiety Story – How I Recovered From Anxiety, Panic, and Agoraphobia (My First Book)

https://theanxioustruth.com/mystory

Books by Dr. Claire Weekes and Other Excellent Authors

https://theanxioustruth.com/shop

Table of Contents

References

Cognitive Behavioral Therapy And Variants Thereof

Just about every word I say or write on the topic of anxiety and anxiety disorders is based on the principles of Cognitive Behavioral Therapy (CBT) or its variants. This includes Acceptance and Commitment Therapy (ACT), Dialectical Behavioral Therapy (DBT), and Rational Emotive Behavioral Therapy (REBT).

Throughout this book, I have referenced the long, real-world track record of this approach to anxiety and anxiety disorders. These are the therapeutic systems and modalities I am talking about.

This family of therapies focuses on faulty and unhelpful ways of thinking and behaving. Rather than focusing on particular symptoms or deeply hidden causes for anxiety and fear, cognitive/behavioral models focus on observable, changeable thought, and behavior patterns. These are "active" therapies that require that therapist and patient work together on tasks designed to uncover negative thought and behavior patterns, then to change them. The basic premise is based on the idea that people can learn new ways of thinking and behaving that allow us to experience our problems in a new way with more desirable outcomes.

I make it a habit to remind people that I have not invented any of this. The information and guidance I provide are based primarily on these tried and true interventions that have been used to successfully treat anxiety and anxiety disorders for decades all around the world.

I'm sometimes asked if the Claire Weekes's[1] approach to anxiety (I give full credit to Dr. Weekes as one of the foundational sources for all my work) is CBT. The answer is that the approach she and now I advocate is based heavily on the principles of CBT and its variants. While she never specifically wrote CBT handbooks or workbooks, it is true that the notion that you can learn new ways to experience your anxiety and its symptoms squares directly with the foundations of CBT and related therapies.

These therapies have roots tracing back into the 1920s and the research done by John Watson in behaviorism and its potential applications. While early forms of behavioral therapies were based primarily on the tenets of classical and

1"Claire Weekes," Wikipedia (Wikimedia Foundation, May 20, 2020), https://en.m.wikipedia.org/wiki/Claire_Weekes

operant conditioning, the current generation of CBT and its variants incorporates aspects of learning theory and cognitive theory. When you hear me talk about your anxiety issue as a bad mental habit that can be unlearned, you are hearing the echoes of both learning and cognition research that has been carried out since the 1950s and 1960s, and that continues today.

Many people will recognize the names Aaron Beck and Albert Ellis. These pioneering behavioral scientists are widely regarded as the "fathers" of modern CBT and its variants.

The internet is full of excellent resources should you want to learn more about the origins of CBT and its foundational concepts. A good place to start to understand how CBT evolved and how it relates to psychodynamic and humanistic forms of therapy is this synopsis found at *Psych Central*:

https://psychcentral.com/lib/the-origins-of-cognitive-behavioral-therapy/

A Brief Word About Belief, Understanding, and Overthinking

Before we get started, I need you to understand that for what I am sharing with you in these pages to work; you don't have to believe what you're about to read.

You've likely been told that you can get better, but thus far, that hasn't really worked out, so I realize that you might be short on belief.

That's OK right now. It's enough that you are here.

A ton of information is about to come your way. I get it if your brain isn't exactly in a receptive state right now. You only have to do your best to take in the information, then give it a try. Even if you don't believe or don't fully understand the magnitude of it yet, just trying is enough to get things moving in the right direction for you.

Don't forget; you can always circle back and re-read.

I designed the book to be used that way. So that you can read it multiple times, allowing each lesson to stand alone.

Many people find that they don't fully buy into the process until after they start using it anyway. So if you're not sure that you can put all your eggs in this basket just yet, that's fine.

I'd also like to address the issue of overthinking.

If you're reading this book, there is a chance you might call yourself an overthinker. Many people who develop anxiety disorders fall into this trap. As you read, I ask you to resist the urge to pick apart every word and phrase. I cannot explain everything at once, but I have done the best job I can.

My process when writing is that I have to follow a logical sequence. So when you run across a concept that seems unclear or incomplete, highlight or underline it, then keep reading. There is a very good chance that I will fill in the blanks for you a lesson or two down the line. Do your best to get through the whole guide first and make it all the way to the end to ingest as many of the lessons possible. Don't let one unclear or "triggering" idea throw you.

You may get confused or even a bit intimidated by what I'm going to say. Keep going. I know you can do it, even when you are feeling uncomfortable about what you're reading.

What I'm going to tell you helped me. It has literally helped millions of others, and I know it can help you. When you get discouraged or want to bail, remind yourself that you are worthy of making the effort to learn a new way and build a better life. I know you're worth it. I want you to remember that too.

Finally, I designed this book as a classroom. It's been written in a particular sequence to take you from anxious, afraid, confused and lost, to hopeful, knowledgeable, and confident in the direction you must go. Go all the way through the chapters and the lessons in the order I've presented them. Once you've done that, you can go back and skip around to focus on particular lessons when you need them most, or to clarify the things you are unsure of. It will help for you to see the entire picture before picking and choosing the things you want to focus on.

Introduction

I was you. I was afraid, anxious, lost, confused, and totally unsure of where to turn to solve my anxiety problems.

I was crippled with panic disorder, damn near stuck in my house because of agoraphobia, and afraid to be alone for even a minute for fear that I might panic and need to be "saved."

I didn't drive on the highway.

I didn't go to my office (even though I owned the company).

I was afraid of my phone ringing because it might mean I would be required to do the things that scared me so much.

I spent all of my time focused on my body and mind. *How am I feeling? What is that twinge, tickle, pain, tingle, or change in temperature? Are my eyes working? Is everything suddenly blurry?*

It felt so often like my legs weren't there. I couldn't watch the news, or action movies, or hear anything at all that referenced death or dying in any way. Something as simple as the sun going behind a cloud would send me into a panic.

I was unable to drive my kids to events. I was allowing my business to crumble beneath me, and I was generally failing at life, all because I was afraid.

And I was afraid all the time.

I was you at three different times in my life.

But now, I am not.

I am fully recovered from my anxiety disorders and living a normal, happy, productive life free from irrational fear and worry.

Since recovering, I have spent quite a bit of the last 12 years or so helping other people do the same.

I've done this in various internet forums and on message boards.

I've spoken to hundreds of anxiety sufferers directly and become friends with many of them. I've watched people struggle, and I've watched people get better and get their lives back.

I've blogged.

I've made videos on YouTube.

Primarily though, for the last five years, I've hosted The Anxious Truth (https://theanxioustruth.com), a podcast about anxiety, panic, and agoraphobia. My podcast has gotten quite popular over time and has even spawned a large and vibrant social media community around it.

I spend a tremendous amount of time reading about this issue, learning about this issue, staying abreast of research in the behavioral sciences, and relaying what I know—and what I 've learned from my own experiences—to others around the world. I love doing this thing. It makes me feel that my suffering had a purpose.

If you'd like to read the story of how I recovered from my anxiety disorders, my first book shares that. *An Anxiety Story: How I Overcame Anxiety, Panic and Agoraphobia* was published in February of 2020. It's available at https://theanxioustruth.com/mystory in multiple formats, including a free e-book. It's a short read, but it will tell you who I am and what I've been through.

What I'm going to tell you in this book isn't coming out of thin air. The information is all based on sound clinical practices in psychology and the behavioral sciences, and on my own personal experiences. In this book, I am going to ask you to face your fears directly, as this is the path to recovery and the life you so desperately seek.

It sounds scary and incredibly difficult.

It is both.

But I am not going to ask you to do anything that I haven't done myself. I have been where you are, several times in my life. I know what it feels like and what you're up against, but I also know how to solve your problem because it was my problem, too.

I was you. Now I'm not. If I do my job well with this book, one day, you'll be able to say the same to someone else.

Who Is This Book For And How Will It Help?

This book is written for anyone suffering from repeated panic attacks, agoraphobia, monophobia, and other anxiety-related problems. It is written for the person who is anxious and afraid but also confused as to why all this is happening and totally lost as to what to do to make things better.

This book has five primary goals:

To teach you what the actual nature of the problem is and how you got there. You will no longer be confused.

To teach you that you are not broken or ill and that you can recover from your anxiety problems. You will no longer feel hopeless.

To teach you what is required to recover. You will no longer be lost.

To teach you how to make a recovery plan that will solve your anxiety problem. You will have a clear direction to move in.

To teach you how to execute that plan and move forward toward a better life. You will take real steps toward solving this problem that has plagued you and made your life so difficult.

CHAPTER 1

HOW DID YOU GET HERE?

Lesson 1.1

You Are NOT Broken

You're anxious, afraid, confused, and lost, but you are NOT broken or damaged.

You are not ill.

You do not have a disease that needs to be cured.

You are not imbalanced.

You are not incompetent.

You are not a lost cause.

You are not worse than anyone else with the same problem.

Your situation is not special, unique, or un-fixable.

You are still a complete human being with all the skills and qualities needed to get out of the mess of anxiety. There IS a way out, and you can get there.

Millions of other human beings before you have been in your exact position. Regular people just like you turned things around. They got good advice, pointed themselves in the right direction, then made a plan and executed it.

They found courage when they needed it.

They found determination.

They found persistence.

They found inspiration in the stories of those who came before them.

They discovered strength, learned new life skills, and along the way, uncovered qualities they never dreamed they had.

These humans, from all around the world, are just like you. They were once afraid, confused, and lost. Just like you. But now they're not, and you won't be either.

Solving this problem isn't easy because some hard work is involved, but you are capable of hard work.

Before we move forward together, I need you to believe that this is not your fault, you are not broken or hopeless, and that you already have everything inside you that you need to make your way back to the life you so desperately want. That's the first step of the hard work.

Your first panic attack was awful. It put you on a path into the great unknown. With no education on the real nature of anxiety, panic, fear, and cognition, you had no idea what was going on or why. I know this because this also describes my first panic attack.

Nobody ever told you about panic attacks. There was no semester spent on anxiety and anxiety disorders in middle school health class. Your parents never sat you down and gave you "the talk" about anxiety. For all intents and purposes, you were blindfolded, driven down the highway for a few hours, then kicked out of the car at 100 MPH without a map or a compass. Good luck with that!

Panic seems like a body problem. After all, your body gets completely lit up with all kinds of nasty sensations when you're anxious. *This must be a physical thing, right?* It would seem logical to approach this new situation at face value. "My body is freaking out, so I must work on my body to stop this from happening!" Nobody would blame you for taking that approach.

First stop...*Google. Let's figure this out!*

"What are these horrible feelings I'm experiencing?" "Why is my heart racing?" "Why do I feel so dizzy?" "Why do I feel like I'm going to pass out or die?" "Why is my stomach trying to kill me?"

After the Googling come the rampant thoughts:

Why do they happen?

This is so scary, and I hate it!

How do I stop it?

Nobody would blame you for asking those questions. They seem to be the right questions to ask, and sometimes you feel like you MUST keep asking them to remain safe. This is a common error, although completely understandable.

But sadly, Google likely became more of an enemy than a resource to you. You might have found lots of excellent information about your problem online, but most of it was completely drowned out by some horrible stuff. You probably found a ton of YouTube videos talking about anxiety and how to "fix it." Blogs. Forums. Healing guides. If you were like me, you got buried in an avalanche of dietary advice, exercise programs, crystals, positive affirmations, hypnosis, herbs, supplements, detox programs and endless discussions of "self-care," lifestyle changes, and toxic relationships.

The solution you were looking for was seemingly everywhere, in every direction. You were told that it was what you ingest, what you breathe, *how* you breathe, how you *don't* breathe, who you hang out with, who you sleep with, your job, your boss, your career uncertainty, your finances, your exercise routine (or lack thereof), your non-existent spirituality, being a people pleaser, not setting boundaries, being too rigid, being too unstructured, bad sleep hygiene, leaky gut syndrome, Mercury being in retrograde...and your mom. I can go on and on. But you get the idea.

Maybe you started talking to your friends and family about your anxiety. Perhaps you went online and asked total strangers on Facebook what they thought. Either way, if you spoke to 500 people, you've likely heard at least 250 variations on an anxiety "cure," and you've probably tried at least 200 of them to no avail.

Imagine trying to shoot an arrow at a target, except there are 50,000 targets in your field of view, and they're all moving at all times. *Where do you aim? Everywhere? Nowhere?* All the while you're trying to decide, your body is in an uproar. Your nervous system is locked into high gear. You're continually anxious and often downright terrified. Instead of pursuing actual solutions, you find yourself spending more and more time trying to figure out how to just get away from it all.

Your anxiety and panicking were supposed to be getting better, but no matter what you tried, or which direction you ran, it got worse. Your world got smaller and harder to navigate.

Are you relating to what I'm talking about?

Now, let's talk about horror stories. The more you searched for answers, the more horror stories you heard. How many people did you encounter—especially online—who did nothing but talk about how terrible it is? How many different anxiety symptoms did you read about? How many people did you find who were engaging in an endless cycle of commiserating and comparing stories of failure and hopelessness? How many times have you been told that the best you could hope for was to "manage the disease," medicate your way out of the mess, and just deal with the side effects?

I've heard it all.

Trust me, I know how discouraging and disheartening that discussion is.

So is it any wonder that you're anxious, afraid, confused, and lost? You're precisely where any intelligent human being would expect you to be right now. You had no roadmap to follow. You've been given way too much wrong and inconsistent advice, and you've been drowning in the nightmares of other anxiety sufferers.

There's no mystery as to how you wound up anxious, afraid, confused, and lost. You are a well-designed, intelligent human being. You were responding to fear and discomfort in precisely the way you were designed, and exactly the way everyone would expect you to. That's not broken or ill in any way, is it? It's simply misguided. That's fixable, so let's get to work!

Lesson 1.2

A Natural Process Gone Wrong

Anxiety is NOT a disease.

I don't care what you've been told. You are not sick. This is not an illness, mental or otherwise. If you're offended by this because you feel that the term "mental illness" is an accurate description of why you can't solve this problem or build a better life, then this might be a good time to stop reading. I'm not going to entertain the idea that you the victim of some kind of illness because I know you are not. Humor me. Imagine for a minute that you are NOT actually damaged or sick. Imagine that you can actually get better, then let me show you why this is true.

A disease is what we call it when biological processes beyond your control bring about detrimental changes and/or impairments in the way your body functions at some level. Cancer is a disease. Alzheimer's is a disease. ALS is a disease. You could probably argue that even the common cold is a disease. But anxiety? That's not a disease.

Now that we've gotten that out of the way let me explain what anxiety really is.

Anxiety is a state. It's predictable, regular, natural, and does not indicate defect or malfunction. In a state of anxiety, your body is operating as it's been *designed* to work after millions of years of miraculous engineering—otherwise known as natural selection. Anxiety is the state you enter in response to an imminent threat, real or perceived. It is a close relative of fear—another natural state and is often a precursor to fear. Sometimes, it's difficult to tell anxiety and fear apart.

The physiological hallmarks of an anxiety state are all quite well-known and easily measurable. They are not a mystery. And I want to stress again; they do not indicate that anything is wrong, broken, or malfunctioning.

These are some of the physical manifestations of anxiety. Which symptoms do you relate to?

- Your heart beats quickly. This is normal in an anxiety state.
- You feel dizzy. This is normal.
- You feel shaky and weak. This is normal.
- Your vision gets strange. This is normal.

- You feel hot and/or cold. This is normal.

- You feel short of breath. This is normal.

- Your stomach churns, and you feel nauseous. This is normal.

- You feel an intense need to find a bathroom. This is normal.

- You feel driven to run or escape. This is normal.

- You feel an overwhelming sense of doom.

THIS. IS. NORMAL.

I can go on and on. The internet is awash in large lists of the "top" anxiety symptoms. You don't need me to list them all for you, and I couldn't even if I tried. There's always another symptom anyway. The point is that every last one of the sensations you feel when anxious is entirely normal and expected from a properly functioning human body.

I know you're convinced your most disturbing and scary symptoms are unique and special. You're sure that nobody else feels it as strongly as you do. *This just can't be normal! Something must really be wrong because it FEELS so much like something is wrong!*

Let me address those thoughts right now.

You are absolutely and completely wrong.

What anxiety and panic "feel like"...don't matter.

How you feel – aka the sensations and thoughts you experience — do not matter. I know this seems crazy to you, but you will learn as we go forward, that the feelings are not the problem. They are VERY real, but they aren't the actual problem. How you interpret them and react to them is the problem. Let me repeat for you that I absolutely know that the sensations are REAL. It's just that the danger you think they represent is not.

I promise, we will get into great detail about this later on, but I needed to put this concept out there now because it is THAT important.

And because it is THAT important, I share more on this— much more—later. So, make sure you keep reading. For now, let's get back to the topic at hand.

Anxiety is NOT a disease.

OK fine. It's not a disease. But obviously, SOMETHING is wrong, so what is it?!?!

Fair question. Let's break things down a little. We need to identify the components of this problem you want so desperately to solve.

First, there are the feelings and sensations that you hate so much. These are the symptoms of anxiety. You just read my rant about this. These are *normal* physiological operations in a *healthy human body*. The sensations and symptoms you dislike so much are simply your body reacting as it's been designed to respond in the presence of an impending threat. When needed, your body protects you and prepares you for battle or escape by entering an anxious state.

Sometimes, this mechanism gets triggered at the wrong time. The anxiety/fear response kicks in even when there is no current or pending threat in the environment. You were fine one minute, then convinced you were dying or going insane the next. Maybe that was your first terrifying experience with panic. This happens to almost everyone at least once in a lifetime. Call it a bug. A defect maybe. A design flaw. Whatever it is, it happens...*all the time*. The natural protection mechanism built into your body fired when it shouldn't have, and maybe you found yourself at dinner with a friend, absolutely terrified for no reason.

That is not fun, but it's still not a disease, and it's *still not the problem*.

The problem is what happened after that. You were afraid and did not want to be afraid again. You were uncomfortable and did not want to be uncomfortable again. You interpreted this misfire as something to be avoided at all costs. This interpretation turned your natural threat protection mechanism into a threat! Your brain turned your own normal, healthy body into your enemy.

Once this happened, it was game over. You were locked in the cycle of fearing the next episode, living in a state of high alert, and dreading every tiny hint that it might be happening again.

You were afraid, so you learned to be afraid of being afraid. Does that sound like a disease?

Once you are living in a constant state of worry, always on guard for the next wave of anxiety symptoms or panic, then you are breeding the very thing you dread. Your fear manufactures tension, anxiety, and MORE fear. By teaching yourself that you must avoid and escape those feelings, you've created a monster where none previously existed.

Do you see now why your anxiety is not a mental illness? Can you see how the situation you are living in today is simply the result of a natural process gone awry? This is not an illness. You are not broken or damaged. You just learned some incorrect lessons. Your anxiety is nothing more than a collection of bad brain habits.

That doesn't sound so bad, does it? Habits, no matter how bad, can be broken. Things you learned in error, that you thought to be true all this time, can be unlearned and corrected. You are not sick, ill, or full of disease. You just need to fix some mental mistakes, that's all.

Have you ever spent years singing along with a favorite song, only to learn that you've been singing the wrong lyrics? For God knows how long you were convinced you knew the words, until one day you found out that everything you thought you knew was wrong. This is the same thing. You've been singing the wrong words. Now you can learn the right words and sing them. Much better, right?

Lesson 1.3

Nobody Ever Told You

Let's talk for a few minutes about the severe lack of mental health education and information you've been given most of your life. It's a thing. And it's contributed to where you are today.

In the US, at some point in our formal education, we get basic training in what we call "health." The curriculum includes things like drug and alcohol addiction, use of tobacco products, cancer detection and prevention, safe sex, and how to brush your teeth properly. All valuable for sure. And yes, please clean your teeth after every meal. *See? Free dental hygiene advice, too. You're welcome.*

As of 2018, precisely TWO American states (New York and Virginia) have decided that mental health issues should be included at various points in the journey between kindergarten and high school graduation. If you're living in another country and are unaware of the number of states in the US, we have 50 states. *Two* have taken action to include some primary mental health education. That's not a good percentage. It's a start, but as you can clearly see, we have a very long way to go.

Our formal education system has failed to provide primary education when it comes to mental health, but what about your tribe? Your parents. Your family. Your friends. Surely they were a good source of information and advice.

I think you already know what I'm going to say next. Collectively, from an educational standpoint, your tribe has been no help whatsoever.

The people close to you surely love you and care about you, but they've likely spent more time discussing video game cheat codes with you than helping you understand fundamental human issues like anxiety, stress, fear, and depression. You can't blame them, though. Where would they have gotten the information? We already know that our schools aren't overflowing with it. The internet is mostly a dumpster fire when it comes to this topic, as I touched on earlier and will touch on again later. While I'm sure your loved ones would have wanted to pass along useful information and advice, they had very little chance to get it themselves, so how could they?

The problem you're facing—the thing you're trying to change—is well understood in behavioral sciences circles. Really, it is. If you're in the grips of recurring panic attacks, panic disorder, agoraphobia, GAD (generalized anxiety disorder), or most anxiety disorders, the mechanism of action is pretty well documented, and effective treatment is available. I am not claiming that we know all there is to know about human emotions or the human brain in general. Hardly. We really know very little. But at least when it comes to the nuts and bolts of cognition and learning as it relates to developing and treating phobias (if you are afraid of how you feel, then this qualifies as a phobia), we're in decent shape.

The issue here is that nobody ever taught you about these things. You may be familiar with names like Pavlov and Skinner, or maybe you're into self-help and have heard names like Maslow or Jung, but that's about it. The fact that there is an entire population of smart people who devote their lives to understanding these problems and treating them is mostly unknown. We all know that scientists are working to prevent and cure cancer. We know that drug companies spend vast amounts of money developing new drugs to treat diseases (this isn't a disease—see Chapter 2). We all hear about incredible advances in health like cybernetic prosthetics and cochlear implants for the hearing impaired. But we rarely, if ever, hear anything from the behavioral sciences concerning their advances, even though a TON of great work is happening there.

Let me clarify a little something about the internet.

The internet has changed the world. You can argue whether the change has been positive or negative, but it is a change, nonetheless. One of the most significant changes of the last 25 years has been the spread of information. There is a literal tsunami of words, images, and videos related to mental health issues on the Internet. The problem is that very little of it relates to the behavioral sciences in any meaningful way. We default to emotional and spiritual matters. We fill our social media networks with inspirational memes and quotes. We write blog posts about finding peace and being enlightened and how journaling changes everything. We fill the internet with stuff that kinda makes us feel good to read, and maybe gives us hope in some way. This is great, but in the end, it tends toward the fluffy, the basic, and the non-actionable.

Thank you, internet, for the pretty pictures and Zen quotes, but what do I do when I feel a panic attack coming on? (Spoiler alert...it's not counting all the blue things you can see or singing along with the radio.)

We love easy things. We hate hard things. And let me be brutally honest here, what you're going to do to solve your problem isn't glamorous or easy in any way. It's rote. It's simple. It's almost spartan. It doesn't lend itself to memes and sharable quotes. It's based on very dry science that nobody wants to read. Well, except me. I like to read it. I'm strange that way.

What I'm saying here is that while the path from panic to peace is well-defined, it's not exciting or quick, and it involves doing things that you won't want to do. Nobody wants to read about that.

But there are others like me out there talking about taking a cognitive behavioral approach to anxiety problems. Still, we are hard to find because most people would share a picture of Morgan Freeman saying something he never actually said before sharing an article about the effectiveness of graduated exposure therapy. That stuff gets hidden in obscure corners of the web.

While good information about this problem may not be easy to find, it still exists. We know quite a bit about how this problem occurs and how to fix it. Let's take a basic look at this.

Human beings are subject to stress. We get anxious. We get afraid. Sometimes we get sad and even depressed. This is part of life standing upright at the top of the food chain on this planet of ours. You cannot avoid these things. Our responses—especially to stress, anxiety, and fear—are not mysterious. When studied across large populations, we can see what happens when we worry, and when we are afraid. There are patterns. They are predictable. The good news is that you work the same way that every other human being works.

To solve this problem we're talking about, there are basic concepts to learn and understand. Some basic skills and strategies need to be learned and practiced as part of the process of overcoming your anxiety issues. They will likely be new to you. Even though all humans can benefit from knowing these things, we don't teach them in our schools; we don't teach them in our families, and we don't talk about them enough in our global electronic conversations.

So I will remind you again...this is not your fault.

The information you need to change things is out there. Nobody ever told you about it, and it's pretty hard to find.

Let's fix that.

Lesson 1.4

Adrift In A Sea Of Bad Information

First, nobody told you.

Then EVERYBODY wanted to tell you.

You have likely been adrift in a sea of wrong information. Horribly wrong information. Like, you can't even fathom the epic badness of the information you've probably been given. Thank you, internet!

It's 100 percent predictable that a person who begins experiencing anxiety and panic will start a furious, almost obsessive search for information on every symptom, sensation, and change of bodily state. There's a pattern. Almost everyone follows it perfectly. It happens—that thing you hate. You try to shake it off, but you're worried. Then it happens again. Now you're focused on it. Then it happens again and again. Then anxiety and panic becomes an actual problem, and you decide that it's time to find out what's going on.

You sit yourself down in front of "Doctor Google" to begin your search. The result is a swirling quagmire of misinformation, misapplication of good science, questionable science, BAD science, outright quackery, made-up stuff, and non-actionable fuzzy platitudes. This is just the tip of the iceberg. Next comes the firestorm of bloggers, vloggers, and other "influencers." They have decided that anxiety is an excellent topic to attract likes, views, and attention. What they actually have to say about anxiety is irrelevant. It doesn't matter if it's valid, helpful, or in any way applicable to solving the problem of a full-blown anxiety disorder. Just watch them, please. Because, well, they are influencers! Again, thank you, internet.

As if this isn't enough, you next encounter a wide range of people trying to make money in the anxiety space. In this wave, you're drowned in books, audiobooks, e-books, courses, classes, weekend retreats, and coaching services. When the first wave recedes, the next holds the homeopathic remedies, natural cures, herbs, minerals, crystals, oils, plant extracts, and discount codes for eye of newt.

Finally, when you think you've got your head back above the water, in come the tappers, neuro-linguistic programmers, inner child advocates, chakra clearers, astrologers (yes, astrologers), smudgers, reiki practitioners and re-aligners of meridians. And hypnotists. Oh, the hypnotists!

Let's keep going. There's magnetic cranial stimulation, burning of sage, bobbing your head while breathing, adrenal support, ashwagandha (I just like saying that), subliminal/binaural audio reprogramming, veganism, ketogenic diets, brain wave re-adjustment and...not kidding...primal screaming. If you've been at this for any amount of time, you know that while I'm being a bit ridiculous, I'm not in any way exaggerating. If you can imagine it, it's been held up as a solution to your anxiety and panic problems.

Look, I'm not saying that all these things are totally useless in life. Some people love tapping. Some swear by smudging, and others will give up their crystals only when you pry them from their cold, dead hands. That's fine. If something brings you enjoyment or comfort, then go with it.

However, none of these things is a cure or "fix" for an anxiety disorder. Before we move on, I will simply ask this. *If you believe that hugging your inner child (for instance) has fixed this problem for you, then why are you reading this book?*

The array of "cures" is dizzying, disorienting and disheartening, especially if you've tried many of them without success. If you've been down that road, you know what I mean. After you've been excited, then disappointed for the 10th time, it can be easy to conclude there's no hope. This is all too common, but if you're reading right now, then believe me when I tell you that there *is* hope. Giant bundles of it. I promise.

Now, let's talk for a few minutes about misinformation and questionable advice from the people you actually know and love in real life. This is also a thing. I think it's safe to assume that your friends and family love you and want you to feel better and live a happy life. They always mean well, however sometimes those closest to us accidentally land the hardest blows when it comes to this topic. Bad advice on a personal level tends toward more practical, oversimplified suggestions that can really harm your confidence and your overall outlook.

Have you ever been told to "just get over it"? That one is always fun. "Pull yourself together" is another common one. I've heard of people who have been told they simply need a vacation or more sleep. Friends and family members might suggest that you find a hobby, change careers, or break up with a lousy partner. Get a pet. Move out of that horrible apartment you're living in. Find a boyfriend/girlfriend. Watch a funny movie. These are all actual suggestions you may have heard from people close to you. Again, they mean well, but I understand how difficult it is to listen to such advice.

After all, if you could "just get over it," you would!

Allow me to address one other source of information. I know this is a sensitive topic and that you might feel some relief turning to your faith. I want to say I am respectful of everyone's faith. If you find strength in your faith and religion, there's nothing wrong about that. In my years of interacting with people who have this problem of ours, I have come across many who have told me that they have experienced two primary faith-based issues. The first is that they are concerned that a given recovery plan will conflict with the teachings they hold dear. The second is that they may be in a crisis of faith because they've been told that a higher power will take away the problem. Often they've been counseled by a trusted and loved priest or clergyman, yet the problem persists—thereby causing the crisis of faith. I understand how difficult these issues must be. If your faith plays a significant role in your life and the life of your family, then you are likely looking for a recovery path that will compliment your beliefs and will not run counter to advice you've been given through that channel. I can only tell you that while I may not share your exact religious beliefs, I do think that whatever process placed us here has imbued us with many gifts.

Gifts of reasoning and critical thinking. The gift of adaptation. The gift of flexibility. The gifts of courage and inner strength. The gift of learning. Consider that the path we will be examining together is based on all these things. You will use the gifts you have been given to change your situation for the better. It will not be easy. It requires action on your part. You must carry this weight and do the work for yourself. But what you find when you get down the road is so worth it. If you believe that you have been given this life by a loving creator, consider that He would be joyful watching you utilize your gifts to build a better life for you and the people who love you.

You've now read approximately 5000 of my words. What have we accomplished? We've seen that you are not at fault for where you are right now and that you are not broken, damaged, or diseased. We've established that you've had minimal opportunity to understand the mechanisms at play and that you've been buried in an avalanche of bad advice and wrong information.

It's not all bad news, though. We've also learned that this problem is really nothing more than a collection of bad brain habits learned in times of real but baseless fear. We've seen that this is a fixable problem and that you are in no way beyond hope. You are fixable. This is fixable. And your life can change.

So now what?

Let's layout what this path is going to look like. In the next lesson, I will take you through an overview of what we're going to be doing to enact this change. The good stuff is about to start!

Lesson 1.5

Let's Get Ready To Rumble

Now it's time to start learning and laying the foundation for real change and improvement. I'll lay out exactly what we'll be talking about, what I'm going to teach you, and the impact it will have day-to-day and in the long term.

The first thing we're going to do is to take an in-depth look at the mechanics of anxiety, fear, cognition, and learning. If you're going to change course and start sailing in the right direction, you need to understand what's going on. You don't have to be in the dark about it any longer. It's not rocket science. I think you'll find that the mechanism that got you to where you are now is pretty easy to understand when you strip away all the erroneous stuff you've been inundated with.

We'll discuss how anxiety is just part of being human, and why an anxiety-free life isn't a realistic or healthy goal. We'll spend some time on the idea that your whole body/brain system is working pretty much as designed, just with a few missed turns along the way that require a course correction. I will spend quite a bit of time explaining why this is NOT a body problem and why it most certainly is a cognition and learning problem. Really, you WANT this to be a cognition and learning problem, because that's so much easier to address than an actual physical illness or disorder.

Many many people spend a tremendous amount of time in therapy and engaged in self-examination, hoping to uncover the "root cause" of their anxiety issues. I will explain to you how this is not the best plan to get you back on your feet. It seems like such a logical thing to do, but like most other aspects of this solving an anxiety problem, it's not.

I'm REALLY going to hammer you on two keystone concepts that we will use to build your recovery plan:

1. Attacking your symptoms will not work. Trying to stop the feelings and sensations is a dead end. Examining and explaining them is wasted time and effort. Playing whack-a-mole (Google it) with your anxiety symptoms is a no-win proposition that will only lead to frustration and disappointment.

2. Avoiding is the worst thing you can do. I'm going to show you why avoidance is the kiss of death when

trying to recover from something like panic disorder or agoraphobia. We will talk about why avoiding is the default behavior for the vast majority of human beings, and why you must be committed to doing precisely the opposite of it. That is, it is imperative that you go toward the feelings, sensations, places, people, and situations you fear the most.

Then once we've built a good foundation and understanding of the problem, it's time to start understanding the solution. So much of what we will discuss is easy from a conceptual standpoint, but it's also odd because it *is* counter-intuitive and often goes against "instinct." That just means that we need to spend some time laying it all out so that you can buy into why you have to do what your body and brain are screaming at you NOT to do! If you're a Seinfeld fan, you've heard George revel in "doing the opposite." This is going to be a key concept for you.

We'll spend some talking about changing your focus. That is, making a shift away from always thinking about and evaluating how you feel. This is a difficult state to live in constantly, so realizing that you're doing that and working on moving your overall focus outward a bit will be really helpful. We're going to have to carefully examine the idea of going INTO fear as opposed to running from it. This is really the most essential part of the whole plan, so I will spend plenty of time showing you why this works and why you must do it, even though it is hard. If you're not ready to do hard things, then you're going to be disappointed with the outcome here.

After we get OK with the idea of going toward fear, we'll go over how to make that happen. You'll learn about why your reaction to anxiety and its symptoms is really the issue, and why you'll have to change that reaction. You can't simply go running into the scary stuff without also changing the way you react to being afraid. They go hand in hand as part of the solution. We'll talk about the need to learn new skills that will help you go toward fear with a new reaction. Things like fundamental focus and meditation skills, proper breathing, and on-demand muscle relaxation are necessary, so we'll go over those things. I'll probably rant about the need to continually practice your new skills so that you can get better at them and use them when you need them most. Well, I'll try not to rant, but no promises.

The last step in understanding the solution has to do with persistence and patience. Utilizing what I am teaching you requires both. But finding persistence and patience can be hard to find, especially in the beginning, so I'll also spend some time explaining why these concepts are important. Then when you find yourself struggling, you can refer back to that information for support.

Once we've gained a good understanding of the solution to your problem, we'll move on to actually making a recovery plan. Getting to the place you want to go requires an actual plan. There are many reasons for this. I will go over all of these reasons with you. What you need to know before we get to the plan is that recovery, even with a plan, is difficult and often wildly inconsistent. Why make it any harder than it already will be? Let's just work on making a good plan so that you have a road map to follow.

Be warned. Your plan will be a DOING plan. This is not a thinking or feeling solution. This is a solution firmly rooted in taking action. This is the part where many people lose it, so I'll do my best to explain why you have to actually DO these hard things without spending all your time thinking about them, talking about them, and learning about them. There's not much to learn. I'll teach you; then you'll GO.

I'm going to tell you that your plan has to include arranging your life so that you can do the work that needs to be done every single day with no days off. It's OK to make yourself a priority right now. It will go a very long way toward accelerating your progress if you do. I will address the common objections to this idea, and why we have to throw them out the window. The work will get done every day. We'll talk about how small steps taken repetitively is MUCH better than trying to fix everything in big leaps. This is a common mistake people make, but don't worry. I won't let you make it.

We'll talk about timeframes. I know this is often the million-dollar question. "How long will it take me to be normal again?"

Sadly, I can't really tell you, but we can discuss some average timeframes and the factors that can speed up and/or slow down the process. Having realistic expectations and understanding the need for patience and persistence that I mentioned earlier will really help you.

Once we've got your plan nailed down, we will move onto goal setting. A plan involves setting goals. Otherwise, there is no actual plan. We'll go over how to identify the goals most appropriate for your situation, how to set incremental goals, and how to identify the activities and tasks that move you closer to achieving those goals. Then we'll talk about how your goals will change over time. Your plan will be a living, breathing thing. It will evolve as you make progress. Both the smaller objectives and overall direction contained in your plan will adjust over time. You'll want to be prepared for this. Again, knowing what to expect is a huge help.

Finally, we will move on to actually executing your plan and what that entails. This is where the rubber hits the road. The actual doing part. This is the part where you're picking up new skills, practicing them, and putting them into play as you intentionally do things that presently terrify you. Executing your plan is what creates real change in your life. It's the heavy lifting, and it will be hard, but so worth it.

Executing your plan will involve commitment, prioritization, time management, and working with your family and friends. We need to get them in the loop and on board in whatever way you think is best for you.

We will fill your toolbox with useful tools. I mentioned meditation, breathing, and relaxation. We will go over all of this in detail. We will spend a fair amount of time talking about how you must expect to struggle at times. This is another pitfall for many people, so we have to prepare for that. There will be days when it feels like you are accomplishing nothing, or that you have slid back to square one. I will give you a place to return to when you need to combat those thoughts. We'll discuss how and when to make judgments as to your progress. Above all, we will talk about how progress is never measured by feelings. Progress will be measured by <u>what you do when you're anxious, uncomfortable, and afraid</u>. These are the fires that forge the new you. This is important, so I will spend plenty of time on that topic.

Finally, we will see that as you progress, recovery isn't always all about recovery. You're also living life while you're working on solving your problem. We need to go over how sometimes you just need to live for the sake of living rather than just for recovery. This is a concept that many miss. It's common to get entirely consumed by the recovery process to such an extent that you can lose context and focus. I will give you plenty of material that you can refer back to so we can keep that from becoming a problem.

As you can see, there is much work to do. There are many concepts to cover, lessons to learn, and steps to take. It will be challenging. It will require you to re-think most, if not all, of what you've been doing. It will likely require you to forget everything you think you knew to be true. You will go against what you think is common sense, and you will go against instinct, at least in the beginning. You will learn to think differently about this problem, and you will learn to trust that you've been *designed to recover*.

You will have understanding, direction, a plan, a purpose, and optimism where none has existed. We're going to wipe out that lost and confused thing. Then we're going to take care of the afraid part. When we get there, magic happens.

Ready?

CHAPTER 2:

UNDERSTANDING

THE PROBLEM

Lesson 2.1

Anxiety Is Part Of Being Human

If you are hoping to engineer a life free of anxiety and fear, you need to change your expectations.

That said, this does not mean that you are doomed to a lifetime of horror. Your perception and interpretation of anxiety are warped and distorted at the moment. You see anxiety in ways that other people do not, but that won't always be the case. We are going to unwrap things for you, and it will be awesome.

Believe it or not, anxiety and fear are not your enemies. One day when this is all in your past, you will understand what I am saying. When I find myself anxious, worried, or even a little afraid, it's time for me to stop for a few seconds and ask why. Anxiety and fear have become my tools. They're beacons that help me stay mentally focused. That might sound like crazy talk to you. I assure you that while I may, in fact, be slightly mad, this talk is most certainly not.

Anxiety and fear are part of being human. EVERYONE gets anxious now and then. Anyone who tells you they don't is lying to you and to themselves. Remember that anxiety the way you know it, and anxiety the way other people know it, are not the same thing. For "normal" people (no such thing, btw!), who are not dealing with an anxiety disorder, anxiety can be as simple as a nagging sense of upset or discomfort. Something isn't quite right for them, and they're not sure why. Their discomfort can have a particular source, or it can be very vague and general. There may be worry or even fear attached, but for a typical person, these feelings are not cause for alarm. In the general population, anxiety does not automatically equal a disastrous onslaught of terrifying physical sensations and thoughts. "Normal" people (such a terrible term) have not learned to be afraid of their anxiety, worry, and fear. So what they experience appears to them in a much more acceptable form than it does you. One day, in time and with work, anxiety will appear in a gentler, more acceptable way for you, too.

I know that part of what I just described will resonate if you're dealing with generalized anxiety disorder (GAD). Let me address that quickly. You're thinking about that nagging feeling of being upset and anxious that seems to never go away no matter what you do, right? What's the difference between your nagging, lingering anxious state, and the nagging, vague, amorphous anxious state of the ordinary person? The difference is the reaction. The "normal" person knows they feel this way, but they ascribe no particular importance to it. I'm sure they don't enjoy it, but for some reason, they do not immediately turn inward. They do not grab onto their feelings and ride them around all day. They coexist with their feelings. That's the difference. We will get into how that works later. I just wanted to briefly acknowledge you if you are dealing with GAD.

Let's talk for a few minutes about anxiety, fear, and courage. They often go hand and hand, but not always.

But what is courage? If you think that courageous people aren't afraid, think again. This is a common misconception. Courage is not the absence of fear. Courage is doing what you need to do even though you are afraid of doing it. When I talk about being courageous, I am not asking you to not be scared. I am asking you to act even when you are afraid. Right now, this seems like a monumental task for you. I get it. When I tell you that you will never live an anxiety-free life, you may freak out. You may be wondering how you are going to figure out how to be brave every day forever. Don't worry. That's not what I'm telling you.

I need to repeat that accepting anxiety as a part of life does NOT mean that extreme anxiety, panic, or agoraphobia are unavoidable. While you will experience anxiety and fear while going through the recovery process, you will NOT be required to be courageous all the time for the next 80 years. Not every person that experiences anxiety is mustering up superhero levels of bravery to get through it. I promise that while you'll need to exhibit extreme levels of courage to start, this is temporary. Your excessive levels of anxiety are also temporary. When you get down the road to solving this problem, you will no longer see anxiety as a fire breathing monster that requires epic courage to face. It will shrink and soften, and your courage will surface faster and feel more natural to you. Over time you won't even think about having to be brave anymore. You'll know when the situation warrants it, and then you'll do it.

While right now, you may be focused on nothing but banishing anxiety and fear from your life—because you are understandably desperate for relief—this is an unrealistic expectation. I need you to really work on dropping that mindset as quickly as possible. I need you to trust that anxiety won't always be a monster and that it will be OK for it to be part of your life in the future. Why am I saying this now? At the end of the last lesson, I wrote about how we will work on setting goals as part of your recovery plan, and about how learning how to judge your progress is so important.

Expectations impact goals.

An unrealistic expectation, such as being totally free of anxiety forever, will lead you to set unrealistic, unreachable goals. Unrealistic goals lead to distorted assessments of progress and sometimes mistaken feelings of failure.

I have heard so many people proclaim themselves as "back to square one" after an anxious day. They see themselves as failing at recovery if they experience panic. They have fallen into the "zero anxiety" trap, thinking that the last week or so without a panic attack means they're doing so well. That is not a proper assessment of progress. This is how inaccurate, self-deprecating judgments about your progress come about. We need to set expectations properly now so you can avoid that trap.

Do not expect to be anxiety-free. Certainly not now, and not 20 years from now. Trust that your relationship with anxiety is not going to end, but that it will simply become a far less impactful part of a normal, healthy, happy human life. Expect that you will feel anxiety and panic while on the road to recovery but know that this is VERY different than the gentler form of anxiety and worry you will experience as a typical human being in the future.

Just for a few minutes, stop and imagine the future you. Imagine being a person who understands anxiety and accepts it. Imagine being "that person" who approaches anxiety, not with dread and apprehension, but with wisdom and a willingness to listen to it and learn from it. Imagine that you are at peace with whatever sensations and thoughts may arise on any given day because you are not afraid of them. Imagine a better version of yourself.

You already are that person. You just don't know it yet.

Lesson 2.2

You Are Working As Designed

Before I start this lesson, I want to give full credit and my gratitude to my friend Monique Koven for teaching me the concept I am about to explain. Monique has framed recovery from PTSD and anxiety in a beautiful way. I encourage you to check out Monique's work at cptsdcoach.com. She's a lovely human being.

***

How many times have you heard the statement, "Different things work for different people"?

If you're nodding your head in agreement because you KNOW this statement is obviously true, then you're carrying more baggage than you should while trying to get your life back.

Here's some news. We are all the same, and this is a simple problem at its core.

Yes, I am aware that we all have different backgrounds, different experiences, and different beliefs. We come in different shapes, sizes, and skin tones. We have different genders and diverse religions and economic backgrounds. We speak different languages and have our roots in different cultures and traditions. It's beautiful, isn't it? But let me repeat this. When it comes to how we learn, and the mechanisms of thought, fear, and avoidance, WE ARE ALL THE SAME.

Before you decide that I have no idea what I'm talking about, ask yourself why you feel that way. If you think I'm entirely off base here, what makes you say that? Do you think that your anxiety is unique to you and that nobody else feels what you feel, or thinks what you think? Do you believe that your unique experiences in life have put you in a special place that nobody else has ever been in? Are you convinced that your anxiety, panic or agoraphobia is chock full of subtle nuances that make it unique? Are you sure that your childhood or your past relationships have added dimensions that must be carefully considered before you can get past all this? Do you view your anxiety problems as being based on a complex system of events, triggers, and beliefs? Does a "one size fits all" recovery philosophy seem mildly offensive to you as a unique human soul?

Fair enough. Consider this.

When a person is bitten by a dog, they may develop an intense fear of dogs, suddenly refusing to be within 100 feet of a dog. A person on a very rough flight may develop a fear of flying and never fly again. A person who experiences food poisoning after eating at a particular restaurant will often refuse to ever eat at that restaurant again. Someone who has been in a car accident may afterward be afraid to ride in a car and may insist only upon walking everywhere.

Would life experiences, culture, faith, economic standing, education, or ethnic background enter into these equations? Is a person raised in a loving family less likely to develop a fear of flying after a frightening flight? Is the desire to not repeat food poisoning rooted in anything more than the fact that food poisoning really sucks? A bad experience leads to a persistent fear of repeating that experience.

It's not magic.

Nobody questions this. It happens every day. Nobody would categorize an avoidance of dogs after being bitten as a unique or special situation worthy of some complex consideration. This is a simple learning and cognition problem, not a complex web of experiences and beliefs and tendencies.

Human beings dislike discomfort and fear. We do what we can to avoid those things.

You had experiences with panic and anxiety. You labeled those as horrific and catastrophic. You now have a persistent fear of repeating that experience, and you live accordingly. The mechanism of action is both repeatable and straightforward across large populations. You are where you are today because of a well-known, often observed process of cognition and learning that is essentially the same in all human beings, and in many animals.

We are all the same. When it comes to learning fear-based responses and developing avoidance routines, our brains are all built the same way. This is good news. You are not defective. Your anxiety and panic experiences have left memories. Those memories create thoughts. Those thoughts create sensations and feelings, and those then shape your behavior.

Simple. Normal. Expected.

You are not complicated or unique in this situation. Your anxiety isn't different, nor is your anxiety any worse than

73

anyone else's is or was. We do not have to dig to find out what's wrong with you because we already know what's wrong. Nothing. You are wonderfully normal and, therefore, quite capable of amazing things, including recovery from your anxiety disorder.

You are working predictably and as designed. You've just learned some wrong lessons that you now have to un-learn.

A few basic principles to remember.

1. When you want to counter every recovery suggestion with "BUT ...," you are thinking of your problem as unusual or unique. This is incorrect.

2. When you want to question how such a simple solution could possibly work for you, you are thinking of your anxiety as more complicated than it is. This is incorrect.

3. When you want to say that your thoughts feel so real and that the sensations are scarier and harder to deal with than what others are experiencing, you are thinking of your anxiety as different and worse than everyone else's. This is incorrect.

You're going to have to abandon these things.

I know this may sound a bit crazy or even extremely harsh. If you've wrapped yourself in a cloak of complicated thinking and elaborate avoidance for any length of time, it might seem like I'm asking you to abandon your identity.

It may initially feel like you are somehow dishonoring or invalidating your unique life experiences and your specialness as a human. Trust me; you are not. Let's look at the problem of not being able to get in the car alone (for example).

Your anxiety and the rest of your life are, in many ways, disconnected. From a purely nuts and bolts perspective, one has nothing to do with the other. Of course, the rest of your life matters, but if you look at the act of getting in the car and driving down the road as being no different behaviorally than the act of tying your shoes, you can see what I mean.

It would be best if you accepted that when it comes to solving this particular problem—being anxious, afraid, confused, and stuck—you work the same as everyone else. You must accept that you are working as designed and that both the problem and the solution are simplistic in nature.

If you can grasp this concept and trust in it, you can stop carrying all the added luggage that you think is required for recovery. It is not, and you will really benefit from putting it all down.

Lesson 2.3

This Isn't A Body Problem

Before you go on, repeat after me:

"I feel anxiety in my body, but this isn't a body problem."

Repeat that as often as you must until you believe it. It matters more than you can possibly imagine.

The single biggest misconception surrounding this problem is that it is a body problem.

I assure you; it is not.

You experience anxiety physically, but that doesn't make it a body or physical problem. This seems completely ridiculous to many people, but the sooner you get your head around it, understand it and believe it, the better off you will be.

Let's break it down.

When anxious or in a panic, your body reacts. Your heart races, you get dizzy, your legs feel weak, and you feel disoriented. You may feel short of breath, or like you are going to pass out, or fall down. You may have stomach related issues like nausea or a need to run to a bathroom quickly. At times you may experience depersonalization and/or derealization. Your hands may shake. Your vision may distort, and you may become sensitive to light. Your muscles will tense. You may sweat and feel hot, or cold, or both in alternating waves. Your heart may "skip" beats. These are natural reactions. Together we call them anxiety symptoms. These are all commonly reported, but again, this is by no means a comprehensive or exhaustive list.

In my Facebook group, I sometimes speak a bit dismissively about physical symptoms of anxiety. This is because I've heard hundreds of them over the years, and I know that they're not the problem. This upsets people who believe that they've got some special symptom nobody else has ever experienced. They want to talk about it. Invariably, in a group of over 4000 people, someone else will chime in and confirm that they've also experienced that sensation.

So much for special.

Trust me, none of your anxiety symptoms are unique to you, regardless of what you may be thinking.

The intense inward focus and scanning that comes with this problem can also contribute to identifying symptoms that, when viewed objectively, may not actually be symptoms at all. At my worst, I was constantly chasing little shooting pains, itches, tickles, and twitches from one part of my body to another. I would have described them all as parts of a vast array of anxiety symptoms. Yet today, they simply do not exist. What's more likely? I was magnifying things by being hyper-aware and hyper-focused on my physical state all the time, or my body was doing things that it magically stopped doing when I stopped thinking about them.

These sensations can be intense. They can linger. They can be downright terrifying, especially sensations related to your heart or your breath. A symptom frightens you. You react by bracing in fear. You trigger the fight or flight response in your body. Suddenly the wheels fall off and you're awash in a storm of sensations that scare you to death.

Why does this happen? Well, with sensations come fear, and with fear comes thoughts. Oh, those anxious thoughts:

"What is that?"

"Why is it happening?"

"What if I am dying?"

"Oh no ..."

"On my God!"

"Help me!"

"Save me!"

You know the list. None are pleasant, none are happy, none lead to positive outcomes. None can be reasoned away, no matter how hard you try. Fear fuels the mind the same way it fuels the body. This is simply the way it works.

The really bad news is that once you light the fire, it will burn. Symptoms lead to fear, which leads to anxious thoughts, which leads to more fear, which leads to more symptoms, which leads to more fear, which leads to more anxious thoughts, and the cycle continues.

The bottom line is that you FEEL these sensations in your body so intensely, and at such a deep level, you logically conclude that what you are experiencing must be a physical problem. You logically assume that the way to get out from under this dark cloud is to fix your body.

If I could just find a way to make (insert your scariest symptom here) go away, things would be so much better. Have you ever found yourself thinking that?

How many times have you visited a doctor, or even hospital emergency room, because you were sure that your body needed rescuing and/or treating or fixing? A few times? Twenty times? I've known many people who have visited a hospital once a week because they were convinced there really was something wrong with them. At a logical level, they know there is not, but they can't help it. Despite all evidence to the contrary, they remain convinced that theirs is a problem that doctors, and nurses should address. They often wind up frustrated and angry because they're simply given medications like Xanax and sent on their way. They're told that it's "just anxiety" and there's nothing wrong. But this is not the answer they're looking and hoping for.

So, they persist. Different doctors. Different hospitals. Naturopaths. Homeopaths. Osteopaths. Chiropractors. Neurologists. Endocrinologists. Nutritionists. Psychiatrists. Whatever type of doctor or other health care provider you can think of, the odds are that someone has gone to them for help with anxiety problems.

You've likely been offered medications of various classes, vitamins, minerals, herbs, supplements, oils, and even substances to apply to your skin or inhale. These are all body-centric approaches to the problem because you feel this problem in your body.

"Please fix my body so I won't feel this way anymore." It's a reasonable request, and a logical conclusion to draw, but reasonable and logical do not equal valid or correct. Things are not always as they appear, or in this case, how they FEEL. Yes, you are experiencing anxiety physically, but that does not make it a physical problem.

While we're talking about how this isn't a body problem, I have to address three specific claims and assertions that frost me every time.

1. Your "gut" is not your "second brain." This is a statement seen over and over, usually in places that regularly misquote and misinterpret scientific studies. I guess needing readers is a thing. You will find the neurotransmitter serotonin in your gastrointestinal tract. But this does not imbue your stomach or intestines with the ability to perform cognitive and/or learning and/or feeling functions. That's not how that works, regardless of how it might "sound right." Leaky gut has not caused you to be afraid of your own body and thoughts. Soil deficiencies caused by some vast agri-business

conspiracy does not make you afraid to drive around the block. Far too much time is wasted on that stuff.

2. Cortisol is called the stress hormone because it appears when we are stressed. That does not mean that your cortisol levels are to blame for your panic disorder. Correlation is not causality. And an entire cottage industry is constructed around the HPA (hypothalamus, pituitary, adrenal) axis that will tell you that a wide range of disorders, including anxiety disorders, are based on imbalances and malfunctions on this axis. Curiously, many of these claims are found on alternative medicine websites that also often sell (either directly or through affiliate marketing links) supplements that will "fix" your HPA axis. They can tell you what your problem is, then sell you things to fix it. How...uhm...convenient? Oh, but what they are trying to sell has not been tested or intended to treat any particular symptom or disorder, so....yeah, don't count on that.

3. DNA sequencing is amazing. The ability to map the human genome and deconstruct the double helix of life leads to advances in medical science. None of those advances, however, involve "genetically testing" you for anxiety then prescribing a custom-designed combination of foods, drinks, and supplements that will cure you. I have four letters for that:

S-C-A-M.

OK, that's off my chest!

Remember, your symptoms are physical. Your actual problem is not. The real problem is cognitive in nature. We will cover that in the next lesson. For now, you must understand that even though this mountain of experience all seems to point to this being a body-centric problem, trying to treat it that way is a bad idea. It will almost always lead to disappointment and discouragement. Sure, it's possible that there are body-centric solutions may offer temporary relief of a given symptom, but another symptom will usually pop up in its place. Medications come with side effects and do not work forever. Other body-focused solutions simply don't work at all because they're either ill-conceived or outright scams.

If you've spent any time at all trying to address this problem by adjusting your body, I'm guessing you already know everything you've just read. Maybe you've just been holding out hope that there's a fix you haven't found yet. Bad news. There isn't. At least not one that centers around making changes to the way your body works.

If you're new to this problem, then hopefully, I've managed to save you a bunch of time, effort, money, and disappointment.

Either way, let's move on and take a look at the actual problem. Thinking and learning.

Lesson 2.4

This Is A Cognitive Problem

I think, therefore I am...anxious.

Apologies to my old friend Rene Descartes, but this pretty much sums it up. I might be able to just stop writing here and go lay in the sun for a while, eh?

OK, maybe not. But seriously, this is precisely the problem. As I have told you repeatedly, this is a cognitive problem. This problem that has you at wit's end, afraid all the time, anxious all the time, focused inward and on guard all the time, and possibly living a smaller and smaller life, is a thinking and learning problem. It's not a body problem. Here's why.

It's never how you feel.

I'm going to repeat this.

It's <u>NEVER</u> how you feel.

That's not what matters. What matters when addressing this problem is how you INTERPRET and REACT to how you feel.

I understand that you are drowning in a sea of physical sensations that scare you and make you uncomfortable. Now, I must ask you one critical question because we've hit one of the touchstone concepts of this solution. Other than making you afraid and uncomfortable, have any of those sensations ever done any actual harm? And now that I think about it, there's more than one critical question here. There are a few actually.

Was your body damaged or injured by your anxiety symptoms?

Did you go insane or lose total control of yourself?

Did you die?

Before you answer these questions, there are rules. You may NOT use the phrases "feels like" or "felt like." Those are prohibited words going forward. They are ruining your life. They are your sworn enemies now, and you will not speak them again. Given that rule, go ahead and answer the questions. I'd suggest you grab some paper and a pen and write down the questions with your own hand. Then answer them with your own hand. Again, do NOT use the phrases "feels like" or "felt like." Try not to use the word "but" if you can help it.

You already know the answers to these questions. Nothing happened. You were not actually damaged or injured. You did not go insane. You did not die. You were only uncomfortable and afraid. That's all. Nothing more. Nothing less. You must start telling every panic and anxiety story like this. Anxiety and panic make you uncomfortable and afraid. END of story.

Now let's move on to the next questions. We know you did not die.

Do you think that anything you've been doing while anxious deserves credit for that?

Do you think that staying home saved you from your 200th heart attack?

Did calling your best friend to talk on the phone keep you from losing your mind?

Did racing back home keep your spleen from spontaneously combusting?

Does having your wife in the car with you prevent horrible things from happening? Does she have some kind of supernatural control of your mind and body that exists outside the laws of physics?

Again, these are easy questions to answer, especially while you are calm and collected. Of course, none of your safety and avoidance behaviors have saved you from harm in any way. When you look at your situation calmly and objectively, it even seems a little funny, doesn't it? For about a year, I thought a tin of mints in my car was required to keep me safe. Mints. No kidding. You can't make this stuff up.

So why is this really a cognitive problem? Because you have thought your way into a phobic response to your anxiety sensations. You perceive the sensations as dangerous and a threat. Your brain has mixed up the connection between fear and safety.

Remember this hereafter: they are two different things.

When you watch a scary movie, you can be terrified, but you know you're safe. When you ride a rollercoaster at an amusement park, you can be afraid, but you know you're safe. When you experience anxiety, you are scared, but this time your brain has decided that you are NOT safe. It is taking experiences, extrapolating outcomes that do not exist, and predicting a disastrous future that never happens.

It is mistaken, but your brain is telling you that you are unsafe when anxiety and panic strike. It has been telling you that you must, therefore, avoid those things. *It has taught you to fear how you feel*.

That's a little mind-blowing and it's a huge revelation that will help you get better.

To avoid the perceived danger and remain safe, you have developed an array of safety rituals and avoidance behaviors designed to protect you from those horrible outcomes your brain keeps creating. You need your bottle of water, your phone, your mints, and your safe person. You can't be alone. You can't leave the house, or maybe you can't even leave your bedroom. If you do leave the house, you can't go too far away. You can't be around people. You can't wait in line at the bank. You can't pick up your children from school. You can't go on vacation with your family or visit people around the holidays.

If you do these things, you may experience the dreaded anxiety or even the horror of panic, so your brain has decided to rule them out as ever happening to keep you "safe."

Sorry brain. You've failed the class. You got it all wrong.

This is a cognitive problem because of how you've misinterpreted fear and discomfort as danger. What's worse is that you've been reinforcing the erroneous belief in false danger by avoiding and hiding and escaping. You think these rituals are saving you. In reality, you've always been safe. Afraid and uncomfortable, sure, but safe. All those things you do or don't do to avoid the danger? They're not required. They're useless. They're saving you from exactly nothing because you've never needed saving.

Your brain has reached incorrect conclusions and learned the wrong lessons about anxiety. As a result, your mind has developed some nasty habits.

Since this is a cognitive problem—a thinking and learning problem—there are a few things we need to touch on before moving forward.

You are not afraid of the supermarket (for instance). You are afraid of how you will FEEL when you go to the supermarket. There is a big difference there. You're not scared of leaving the house. You're afraid of how you FEEL when you leave the house. You're not afraid of going to a restaurant. You're afraid of how you FEEL when you go to a restaurant. If we look at agoraphobia, for instance, it's not really a fear of open spaces or a fear of leaving one's home. Agoraphobia is a severe enough fear of your anxiety symptoms that it gets you to change your life to avoid situations that you fear will trigger those symptoms. You're not afraid of the world. You're afraid of how you'll feel in the world.

What you choose to think about and focus on matters. When we understand that the problem is misinformed and misguided fear, then we can make a plan to address that. We will do that in the next chapter, but right now, I want you to understand that what you focus on is essential. You are going to have to stop focusing on your symptoms and how you feel. Training your attention on these things has not and will not help you. I think you will see that if you look closely at the situation for a moment. You also must not focus on specific tasks and challenges. They're all the same. A wedding, a funeral, and a trip to the bank are now all the same task in your world. This is a general problem of misinformed and misguided fear, not a specific problem of being trapped in a conversation with your neighbor at church.

How you talk about this matters.

Just like what you focus on will matter, how you talk about this to yourself and to others will matter. We can now see that we have to work on our fear response—inappropriately triggered fight or flight misconstrued as dangerous. We need to change how we describe this problem in general and how we describe specific events. Think about your current "storytelling" style as it relates to your anxiety problem. Are you talking about working on changing your fear response so that you can fix those lousy brain habits, or are you repeating lists of symptoms and recounting how horrible every panic attack is and how you felt like you were dying? We're going to have to work on this. And you need to know it will matter to your recovery.

This is a thinking problem. A learning problem. You've learned to be afraid of something you don't have to be scared of. You've built an empire of safety and avoidance behaviors. You've developed thought patterns that are keeping you stuck in that cycle of escape and avoidance.

When you were a student, and you took a test, you would get a grade. The teacher would mark your answers as correct or incorrect and would often tell you why you were wrong. You would get your test back, and if the teacher was a good one, you'd have the chance to study your mistakes and fix them. The issue here is that you never got your test back. Your brain got lots of things wrong, but you never knew it and, therefore, never had a chance to fix the mistakes.

Well, you're about to get your test scores. While it might not be pretty at the moment, you'll have much higher grades in your future.

Lesson 2.5

Attacking Symptoms Doesn't Work

It's natural to want to attack the awful sensations that scare you, but that doesn't work. Let me explain why trying to make your symptoms go away is a bad plan that won't really lead to long term change in your life. Remember, I have been there, done that and got the t-shirt.

We've already seen that this isn't a body problem. We've talked about the long list of body-focused fixes and cures that have not amounted to much for you. Still, many continue to focus on symptoms and sensations long after they should have abandoned this approach. Tremendous amounts of time, effort, and even money are spent attempting to address one symptom after another. This will lead you down dead end after dead end. It will eat up time that could be better spent on actually solving the problem. Symptom "seek and destroy" also consumes what I like to call "mental capital."

To overcome this problem, you must have drive, determination, persistence, and courage. Those factors are your mental capital—your cash reserves. You'll draw on these reserves to fund your recovery. Spending time chasing symptoms burns mental capital that would be better spent on other activities and approaches. It will lead you into frustration, disappointment, and even despair. Let's look at a few reasons why attacking symptoms doesn't work.

Attacking symptoms is essentially playing a never-ending game of whack-a-mole. Find a way to knock down one symptom, and another will take its place in short order.

As of this writing, my Facebook group has approximately 4000 members. One of the most frequent discussions in the group is precisely this. A person that has seemingly conquered one symptom suddenly finds that another has taken its place. Sometimes more than one. This is incredibly common. The symptom-centered approach to this problem often leads to life on a never-ending merry-go-round of rotating issues.

It's your heart.

It's your breathing.

It's the pain in your back.

It's the heavy feeling in your legs.

Now it's your vision.

Then it's a headache.

What's this new pain in your left hand?

Why do I have a lump in my throat that I never noticed before?

It's a sudden irrational fear of food allergies that you've never had before.

It's your sleep.

It's fatigue.

It's your heart (again), and the cycle continues.

Find a way to "deal with" one symptom, and four others get queued up and wait their turn. This can become frustrating and discouraging quickly. It often contributes to the mistaken belief that your anxiety is somehow worse, different, or even incurable.

You really do not want to get into a game of whack-a-mole with your anxiety symptoms. And you will not win. Why? Because when you try to address your anxiety this way, you are learning the wrong skills while missing out on the skills that will actually help you find your way out of this mess.

Symptom hunting sharpens your inward focus, which is a step in the wrong direction.

When you're hunting symptoms, you're scanning for them. Pick your current "worst" symptom, and you'll find yourself spending most of your time looking for it. Then you'll spend a chunk of time working on the current fix for that symptom, which will invariably involve continually checking to see if the fix is working.

Did it work?

How's my breathing today now that I've done yoga twice?

The quest to extinguish your anxiety symptom will trap you into looking inward all the time. This will keep you stuck in your preoccupation with how you're feeling during every waking moment.

Symptom eradication means you will take the art of camping inside your head to an even higher level. This is not good. We've already established that this is part of the problem. It's most certainly not part of the solution.

Attacking symptoms reinforces logic errors and creates bad logic habits. The most common is the ever-present false connection between correlation and causation. In Latin: post hoc ergo propter hoc. This translates to "after this, therefore because of this." It's a post hoc fallacy error. It is your enemy.

When I was at my worst, I experienced a panic attack after eating Chinese food. I was sure that whatever was in the food was to blame, so I refused to eat Chinese food for quite some time. I was fixed, until the next panic attack that had nothing to do with Chinese food. See the faulty logic?

I got really good at looking for patterns and connections where none existed. I was a master at drawing flawed conclusions about everything from my blood sugar levels to why I couldn't sleep and why it always felt like I couldn't breathe.

I was wrong about so many things for so long as I chased my tail. Along the way, I was building egregious errors into the structure of my logic and reasoning.

This problem is rooted in irrationality. Weak logic and reasoning skills are the LAST things we need to be building. Focusing on your symptoms will do just this.

Not only does a symptom-focused approach teach you the wrong skills, it literally prevents you from learning the right skills.

Imagine you want to learn to play the guitar. You spend all your time buying different guitar picks, restringing the guitar, tuning the guitar, cleaning the guitar, and fiddling with pedals, effects, and amplifier settings. But you never actually PLAY the guitar.

However, playing the guitar is what you *need* to do—as well as you need to make a ton of mistakes—to learn the instrument.

When dealing with this anxiety problem of ours, we should be learning how to deal constructively with being afraid and uncomfortable. We should be learning how to experience anxiety and panic without reacting as if we are in mortal danger. We should be working on inoculating ourselves against the erroneous phobic response in general.

We should NOT be working on particular sensations and feelings. Learning to drink water, breathing into a bag, or stretching your muscles to make the pain in your chest go away have nothing to with identifying and eliminating the irrational fear response. Attacking symptoms might win you battles here and there, but you will never win the war that way, and that's our goal.

Attacking symptoms will eat up time and effort that would be far better spent learning the skills you need to learn—hard though it may be to do that.

One more thing about attacking symptoms and why it doesn't work. We know that a mistaken belief that this is a body problem logically leads to symptom hunting strategies. What we often overlook is that going on a hard target search for symptoms and solutions keeps you from actually confronting the thing you fear the most—your own fear and discomfort.

It's far easier to shoot at your anxiety symptoms because that doesn't involve facing your fears and going TOWARD the discomfort. Facing your fears is hard and requires doing the opposite of what your survival instinct tells you to do. Give an agoraphobic the choice between getting in the car to drive around the block or ordering a magnesium supplement online. Which do you think the agoraphobic will choose? Symptom hunting is more comfortable than confronting the fear. It's just not effective.

If you've been focused on making the sensations and feelings go away, if you've been shooting at symptoms from the comfort of your safe zone, it's time to make a change. That hasn't helped you, so let's find what will.

Lesson 2.6

Avoiding Doesn't Work

You have likely been avoiding.

You have likely been avoiding places, tasks, people, situations, foods, temperatures, and anything else that you think "causes anxiety."

Panic attack in the car? Stop driving.

Panic in the supermarket? Stop going to the supermarket.

Anxiety in restaurants? Stop going to restaurants.

Eat an apple and feel funny afterward? Stop eating apples.

You are anxious, afraid, confused, and lost, and most of the effort you've been putting in up to this point has been concentrated in one area...avoidance. This has not helped. It's actually made things worse. Avoidance is an evil plan. Most of all, it does not work.

Avoidance comes in many forms. Some avoidance tactics are observable and obvious. Others are subtle and hard to identify. You likely don't even realize that you're avoiding at times, but you are.

Avoidance can take the form of literally going away from or around a challenge or obstacle. This is reactive avoidance. You see a known or potential anxiety trigger in front of you, so you back up or go around it rather than toward it.

When you cancel a lunch date with a friend, you are avoiding. When you turn up the radio or call a friend in response to rising anxiety, you are avoiding. When you tell yourself that you can't go out today because you're feeling bad and need to "be kind to yourself," you are avoiding.

Avoidance can also be proactive in nature. Make a list of the things that "cause anxiety," then search for ways to keep them from ever appearing on your radar. When you spend all your time trying to hunt for and eradicate your anxiety symptoms, you are avoiding. When you Google to find the best supplements for anxiety, you are avoiding. When you won't turn on the television or browse through Netflix because you don't want to hear things that make you anxious, you are avoiding. Even obsessively checking the weather forecast based on a fear of things like snow or heat is a form of attempted proactive avoidance.

Avoidance can also be hidden behind what looks like the exact opposite. The agoraphobic who "can't" drive on the highway or go shopping decides to do these things, but with a safe person in tow. While this may look like forward progress, it is still avoiding to some degree. The driving and shopping are good. The safe person isn't. This is hidden avoidance, masquerading as forward progress.

Avoidance isn't always physical.

You probably spend a tremendous amount of time and effort trying to avoid uncomfortable sensations and physical symptoms.

There's also a fair amount of mental avoidance going on that you may not even recognize.

Anything you engage in for the sole purpose of escaping or drowning out the scary, anxious thoughts is mental avoidance.

When you snap a rubber band on your wrist in response to anxious thoughts and feelings, you are participating in psychological avoidance.

Sometimes mental avoidance—the attempt to drown out or replace fearful and anxious thoughts—exists on its own. If you cannot be in silence except when asleep, this is mental avoidance. Most often, however, mental avoidance comes alongside physical avoidance.

I would like you to sit down for a few minutes and think about what your days look like. This is not an exercise in judging yourself harshly. This is simply an exercise in awareness. If you don't know if you're participating in avoidance, how can you fix it?

Think about all the ways you've engineered your life to try not to feel anxiety, panic, or fear. Be honest with yourself. Do you see all the avoidance behaviors you've been engaging in? You can probably see the overt examples of avoidance in your life but take a few extra minutes and really think about where you might be engaging in the more subtle proactive and hidden forms of avoidance. Gaining awareness and understanding of these behaviors is going to be immensely helpful to you as we move forward.

One more thing before we talk about why avoidance doesn't work.

Realizing what you're doing is a great start, but you really have to OWN what you're doing. You must accept your avoidance behaviors as something that you have chosen to engage in. They were not forced upon you. You must see them as bad habits that are not helping you. In fact, these habits are perpetuating the disorder by feeding the mistaken belief that you must escape anxiety. While avoidance may provide temporary relief, you must accept that in the long run, avoiding will keep you stuck where you are.

So why is avoidance such a bad idea?

If driving on the highway likely means that you will have a panic attack, why on earth is it bad to avoid that? This seems like a fair question but think about what we've discussed in earlier lessons. You are where you are because your brain has learned some incorrect lessons. It has learned to react in fear to things that do not warrant that response. *You have taught yourself that being afraid and uncomfortable is the same as being unsafe, which is untrue.*

This is the cognitive distortion around which your entire anxiety disorder resolves.

When you engage in avoidance behaviors, you are reinforcing that distortion. Go to the supermarket...feel badly. Stay away from the supermarket...feel good. Can you see how this is a detrimental association? You are teaching your brain that the way to feel good is to avoid the supermarket. This is not only untrue, but it sets up a chain reaction of avoidance that quickly spreads into other areas of your life. If you find your world getting smaller and smaller, then you understand what I'm saying.

Avoidance brings reward—feeling temporarily safe and comfortable. Rewards reinforce the behaviors that produce them. This is not always desirable. If your child lies to you to gain a reward, and they get that reward, they learn to lie to you. This is effective learning, but with a less than desirable outcome. If you stay home rather than going to lunch with your friend, you are rewarded with safety and comfort and will learn to do that again. Again, this is effective from a learning standpoint, but is never seeing your friend again the outcome you are after? Since you're reading my words at the moment, I assume it is not.

Feeling temporarily safe and comfortable is an outcome. It is not the best outcome. ALWAYS feeling safe is the outcome we are looking for here. We are attempting to break that faulty link between fear, discomfort, and danger. When we do, you will no longer have to skip lunch to feel safe. You will feel as safe in the restaurant as you do in your bedroom. To get there, we need to teach your brain that those sensations and symptoms you've learned to run from are not dangerous and that even if you go TOWARD them, you will be OK.

Can you learn that by avoiding them? You can read about it. You can talk about it. You can watch videos and listen to podcasts about it. But you cannot learn this lesson without actual experience.

You must go toward the fear to learn these lessons and break the phobic response link. *Avoidance is sending you in the exact opposite direction.*

Avoidance is easy, brings temporary comfort, and leads to more avoidance. Not avoiding is difficult but leads to permanent comfort and real freedom.

Which do you think you should choose?

Humans are creatures of comfort and safety. Avoiding fear and discomfort is natural. As you can see, however, it's the worst thing you can do if real and lasting improvement is your goal.

From a mechanical standpoint, your anxiety problems didn't start with avoidance, but avoidance has been the fuel that has turned a small fire into a raging inferno. You've been trading temporary relief for a long list of restrictions on your life and the fear, confusion, and lack of direction that come with them. If we're going to solve this problem, then you're going to have to understand and accept that while a life of avoidance is more comfortable in the short term, it will not get you to where you want to be. You must be willing to identify and leave your avoidance behind and do some hard things to change your life.

Think about it. Let it sink in. Decide if you're ready to make this move. It doesn't have to be right this minute, but before you read on, you should be on board with this idea.

Lesson 2.7

About The "Root Cause"

Anxiety is NOT an emotional problem.

Before we move forward to talk about understanding the real solution to your problem and making a recovery plan, we need to talk about the idea of the "root cause" of your anxiety issues.

Many, many people spend a tremendous amount of time searching for the root cause of all this nastiness. They dig. They talk. They think. They meditate. They reflect. They dig some more. They may engage a therapist to "work things through." Sometimes there's hypnosis involved or even past life regressions. All are designed to somehow unlock the previously hidden reasons why you are afraid to be home alone in your house.

The search for a root cause seems logical. Surely if you can find out what made you anxious to begin with, and surely if you can take away whatever this was, you'll be fine!

Alas, it pretty much never works that way.

In my direct experience with thousands of anxiety sufferers over the last 15 years or so, I have never seen this happy ending. The digging and probing continues—often for a very long time. Epiphany after epiphany arrives with so much promise.

"Yes! This is it! Now I know why I panic in the car!"

Sadly, two weeks later, you find yourself still wracked with anticipatory anxiety over the thought of making the morning school run with the kids. You still can't imagine attending that family reunion 200 miles away. You achieved such mental and emotional clarity with your breakthrough, but nothing has really changed.

Understandably, this leads to disappointment and discouragement. I've seen far too many people go down this road for too long, only to come to the incorrect conclusion that they are defective and will never get better. It's heartbreaking.

If this sounds like the path you've been on, trust me, it's going to be OK. We're going to get you pointed in the right direction. You're not broken or beyond hope.

Let me say at this point that I am not telling anyone that resolving past issues is a bad idea. It's an excellent idea. If you have experienced trauma in your past or you have unresolved emotional, relationship, self-esteem, or even career issues, it's never a bad idea to work on those. Just understand that if you are dealing with an anxiety disorder, then finding your "root cause(s)" is likely not going to resolve this problem.

Let's look at why.

When you move from anxiety to anxiety disorder—from panic to panic disorder—you have developed a *fear of fear*. You have learned to be afraid of being afraid. The source of your anxiety and panic becomes the anxiety and panic themselves. We described this mechanism in lesson 2.2. Your problem stems from the fact that your brain has learned some incorrect lessons, made some erroneous connections, and developed some nasty habits.

When you veer into "disorder" territory, those erroneous connections in your brain mean that your "root cause"—if there ever was one (and there might not be)— has become disconnected from your fear reaction. If there was a skeleton in your closet that caused those first few panic attacks, it's been replaced by a shiny new skeleton called panic. If there was an original underlying trigger for your anxiety, it's now been disconnected. The anxiety itself is sitting in the driver's seat.

Sorry, Mr. Closet Skeleton. You've been replaced and didn't even get a going-away party.

But why does this matter? It matters because once the connection is made—first between panic and danger, then between driving and panic, for example—the only way to break those connections is through the fantastic process of experiential learning. You *must* experience panic while driving. You must do this without resorting to avoidance, escape, and safety behaviors—to teach your brain a new lesson.

But I'm getting ahead of myself.

We will talk about the process of experiencing anxiety and panic productively in the next chapter. For now, understand that even after you uncover what you are sure was a hidden cause for your anxiety, the wrong lessons and erroneous connections persist in your brain. You have to reprogram your brain before you can go any further. Identifying the root cause – while useful for other reasons – does not help you do that.

While you may find some relief, peace, understanding, and personal growth in your new revelation, that by itself will not rewire your brain and your fear/phobic response. Those responses will remain in place until modified through direct experience.

Imagine that you have piled up some lovely dry branches and leaves, lit a match, and started a roaring fire. Could you put that fire out by blowing out the match you used to light it? This is precisely what you're dealing with now. Your root cause was the match. Your anxiety disorder is the fire. Once the fire is lit, the match no longer matters.

I know this isn't very easy for some people to accept. We are awash in a sea of spiritual, emotional, and personal growth information that tells us that we need to discover ourselves and honor who we are at our core. You have likely been told again and again that enlightenment lies in finding and releasing your fear and your pain. Accepting your past is the only way to leave it behind and grow, right?

You've looked for solace in books and podcasts that revolve around these messages.

You've heard from teachers who repeat these messages again and again.

It seems like common emotional sense to just about everyone. This is why what I'm saying is often met with so much resistance and even disdain.

I assure you that I am not invalidating your emotional pain and suffering. I am not telling you that they don't matter. I am not asserting that your favorite authors and teachers have been doing you wrong. I am not taking away who you are or dismissing your life experiences up to this point.

Your experiences and emotions are valid and valuable, and they should be honored and addressed. I am merely pointing out that if you are afraid to buy groceries alone because you are afraid to panic in the supermarket, then you are beautifully human, and your brain is working like all human brains.

I am pointing out the mechanism of action that has gotten you to where you are now. That mechanism is also beautiful in its own way. *It will get you out of this situation just like it has gotten you into it.*

This is not an all or none thing.

You do not have to choose between resolving past issues and solving your anxiety problem.

You can do both.

Many people do, and many even find that although the two processes may be different, they can be complementary. I've had more than a few people tell me they've actually seen the combined effort to be more rewarding and empowering than they could have imagined.

Before we move ahead with our solution, I'd like you to be OK with the idea that we're not going to talk much about your parents, siblings, ex-partners, or the challenges you've faced in your life.

Instead, we will focus on the mechanics of solving your anxiety and panic problem, and at least within this context, you will need to let that other stuff go temporarily. I promise you won't forget it and that it will still be there when you return to it.

So...let's start working on understanding the solution to this problem!

Lesson 2.8

OCD, Health Anxiety, GAD, and Social Anxiety

I've been speaking and writing on the topic of anxiety and anxiety disorders for quite a few years now.

When I speak or write, I am almost always directly addressing panic disorder and agoraphobia. Most of my references are targeted at those two problems and the issues that surround them. That was my personal experience. These two issues are what I know best.

Over the years, the community around my podcast has grown to include many people who suffer from these problems, but also people struggling with OCD, social anxiety, health anxiety, and generalized anxiety. I am grateful for the opportunity I've had to learn more about these problems.

While I don't claim expert knowledge or personal experience with these issues, I feel comfortable addressing them here. Not because they are completely independent types of anxiety that require their own unique treatments, but because they are *not*.

Each of these conditions has its own set of nuances that demand different types of attention and approaches in some cases, but the core approach to resolving them is the same across virtually every variant. I'd like to address that so that those of you dealing with OCD, social anxiety, health anxiety, or GAD can understand how to apply what you are reading to your situation.

I promise, I care about you if you are dealing with one of these conditions—even if I'm usually speaking from the point of view of a former agoraphobic with panic disorder.

OCD and Health Anxiety

It is often said in the behavioral sciences that every anxiety disorder includes an obsessional/compulsive component. I believe this to be true. At my worst, I developed a clear set of obsessions and linked compulsions that sat comfortably alongside my panic disorder and agoraphobia.

This is quite common with many people.

Panic disorder is about seeking safety from the threat of the next panic attack. The safety is provided by retreat and avoidance behaviors. NOT doing, based on the fear of what feelings, aka "doing," will trigger.

The OCD disorder is driven by the need to remain safe from whatever obsessions have developed. Obsessions vary from person to person, although there are common themes. Obsessions may persist for long periods, or they may change rapidly. Obsessions are focused on an event or condition that we fear will happen based on thoughts we have about those scary events or conditions. This obsession is fed by a compulsion to engage in ritualistic thinking or behavior that we are convinced will prevent those scary things from materializing.

Health anxiety operates the same way. Obsessional fear about health and health-related issues drives, and is fed by, a compulsion to engage in checking, researching, reassurance-seeking, discussing, soothing, and imagined prevention. As in OCD, these compulsive behaviors are described as almost impossible to resist. A person struggling with health anxiety is convinced they MUST engage in these compulsive responses to remain protected against the irrational obsession they've developed over disease, injury, or other health-related matter.

How do health anxiety and OCD relate to my discussion and approach to panic disorder and agoraphobia? They are 180 degrees out of phase. Health anxiety and OCD often generally compel you to DO things, while panic disorder and agoraphobia generally compel you to NOT do things. You can see the contrast here, but the core approach remains the same.

An agoraphobic seeks safety in NOT doing. Avoiding and retreating.

OCD and health anxiety sufferers seek safety in DOING. Checking and monitoring.

A person trying to solve the problem of panic disorder must expose themselves to fear and uncertainty by DOING the things they fear.

A person with OCD or health anxiety exposes themselves to fear and uncertainty by NOT doing the things they feel compelled to do. The mechanism is the same: face fear and uncertainty; make no attempt to save oneself from them, and still wind up OK.

Doing, or not doing.

The exposures may be along opposing vectors, but the mechanism we are leveraging is the same.

If you are reading this book because you are dealing with OCD or health anxiety, your recovery plan will be based on learning to NOT do the things that have been consuming you.

You don't have to practice driving to the supermarket. Doing things isn't really your problem. Instead, you must practice NOT Googling symptoms, or NOT indulging in lengthy inner dialogue centered on an irrational fear of alcoholism relapse (as two examples). Your job is to learn to NOT DO the things that fuel your disorder. See the difference?

The tools we use are the same. Relaxation. Breathing. Learned selective focus. The courage it requires is the same. You're just in the business of learning to NOT do.

Generalized Anxiety Disorder

My listeners and friends who struggle with generalized anxiety disorder (GAD) often point out that panic attacks are not the problem for them. They do not struggle to leave the house, go places, or do things. They struggle with a constant feeling of tension, unease, and fear. They are living life, but they are living it in what they describe as a constant state of anxiety that varies between uncomfortable and borderline unbearable.

If this is your problem, I need to clarify something. People with panic disorder or agoraphobia also often live with a constant background anxiety. Sometimes there is confusion in thinking that between panic attacks, people with panic disorder are anxiety-free. This is not true. This idea leads to thinking about GAD as its own special kind of anxiety problem. GAD isn't panic disorder or agoraphobia. This is true. But it's also not an entirely different species either. A poodle isn't a Yorkshire terrier, but they are both dogs.

While someone with GAD doesn't have specific tasks or places to use as exposure, the approach to GAD isn't all that different than what I will describe for panic disorder or agoraphobia. It would appear that the defining characteristic of GAD and constant background anxiety is not the anxiety itself, but the reaction to it. While the fear of those feelings may not be strong enough to trigger panic or result in extreme avoidance behaviors, the reaction is still one of constant introspection and examination, assessment of condition, bracing, and fighting against the anxious state.

I have yet to find a GAD sufferer that says, "I feel really anxious and uncomfortable today" and ends the statement. Invariably there is an extended narrative about how it won't go away no matter what they try or do. There is insistence that they are not afraid or bothered by it, immediately followed by a demand that it go away. There's a fair amount of disconnect between what a GAD sufferer says about anxiety, and what they do about it.

I will freely admit that while I have lived MANY days where anxiety was with me all day long, I did not have generalized anxiety disorder. My background anxiety was a direct result of panic disorder and agoraphobia. However, I do not have either of those disorders anymore and haven't for many years, yet I can still experience anxious days now and then. I understand what background anxiety feels like. At any moment, many of the people around you are generally anxious. They may be anxious about money, or health, or relationships, or failure, or grief, or any number of problems that humans encounter. The difference between them and you is that they do not attach directly to the anxiety itself. Being anxious is uncomfortable for them, but it isn't a problem by itself. If I have a day where I feel very anxious, I do not leap into action, trying to find out why and thinking of ways to make it stop. Neither do your "normally anxious" friends, family, or co-workers.

In this book, I speak exhaustively about the need to change how we react to our anxiety. These lessons apply to generalized anxiety just like they apply to panic disorder or agoraphobia. You may not have to plan a full set of exposures to get back to school or to walk to the mailbox. For GAD sufferers, exposure happens every time focus gets placed directly on how you feel. Like your friends dealing with panic attacks, you also need to learn to react differently and change your focus. I do not claim to know how to "cure" GAD. I can tell you, however, that the sheer number GAD improvements I've seen created simply by changing the reaction to anxious thoughts and feelings indicates that the approach I am teaching you is valid at its core. Consider this as you read ahead.

Social Anxiety

This is the most difficult topic for me because I have zero personal experience with these issues. I am doing my best to learn from the members of my social media community that struggle with social anxiety issues. Along the way, I have encountered some amazing humans that I have come to admire and respect. Among them is my friend Bethany McLaughlin. She and I have spent quite a bit of time "virtually together" as this book has taken its final form for the last 6-8 weeks. Bethany has taught me many lessons about social anxiety, for which I am very thankful. When it comes to integrating this particular issue with the approach I lay out in this recovery guide, let's let Bethany say a few words about it. Thanks, B!

> *"Recovery from social anxiety is surprisingly similar to recovery from panic disorder and agoraphobia. All the core principles in this book apply: going towards and facing the feared and avoided situations, surrendering to the thoughts and sensations that arise, and changing reactions before, during, and after exposures. A plan can be made to gradually expose yourself to the various situations that you fear. For many people with social anxiety, this could be things like going out in your yard where neighbors can see you, signing a document in the presence of another person, making phone calls, striking up a*

conversation with a stranger, speaking up in a group setting, and so on.

"Social anxiety tends to feel more like a fixture of the personality or as if it's directly tied to one's value and acceptability as a person, and it generally has roots in past experiences of criticism and rejection from other people. This introduces feelings of shame, and shame can be felt and surrendered to in much the same way as fear and panic. Gradually, through exposure and experience, a person with social anxiety begins to learn that their fears are largely unfounded and that even if they do experience judgment or ridicule, any resulting feelings of embarrassment or shame will pass and are not unendurable. Identifying and breaking down false beliefs about yourself and other people should be done, including addressing issues of perfectionism. Cognitive therapy can also be helpful here.

"If you are simply putting yourself through experiences that you find humiliating and agonizing without understanding that your perspective is *distorted, it may be difficult to progress beyond a certain point. That being said, joining and participating in classes or groups, building safe and supportive relationships, and simply showing up more in the world day to day are all wonderful ways of both facing fears and disproving false beliefs, and these experiences alone can go a long way towards your recovery."*

~Bethany McLaughlin, March 2020

CHAPTER 3

UNDERSTANDING

THE SOLUTION

Lesson 3.1

Surrender

I'm going to throw a word at you now that you will probably hate to see. You need to see it and get used to it. This is likely the most important word in this entire book. That word is SURRENDER.

If you've read any of the work of Dr. Claire Weekes, or you've been following my podcast or social media for any length of time, you've heard the words "accept" and "float." I'm not OK with those words anymore. Many of you reading may gasp at this, but yes, I am going to break with our beloved Dr. Weekes here.

We are going to combine "accept" and "float" into one word: SURRENDER.

I'm talking about complete surrender to your anxiety, panic, and fear. This may sound horrifying to you. I understand why. When you surrender to it all, you give up. You stop fighting. You stop resisting. You allow the very worst things you can imagine to actually happen without trying to stop them or save yourself from them. You MUST surrender—give up all resistance—to enact real change. If you continue to fight, resist, avoid, and retreat, you will remain stuck one way or another. I know this sounds harsh, but it is true.

The only way to win this war is to give up the fight. We must give up the fight so that we may learn that we never needed to start fighting to begin with. This is a hard concept to grasp. It requires that you go against every instinct you have to stay safe and protected. Since your brain has constructed a wide range of disaster stories based on your anxiety, panic, and fear, in your mind you will be literally surrendering to things like death, insanity, or total loss of control. This is the part that makes this thing I talk about so simple, yet so hard. This is the part where you need to find your courage. You have that. I know you do. We all do.

You only need to be courageous in the face of allowing IMAGINED terrible outcomes, not actual terrible outcomes. We are not talking about facing certain doom, only imagined certain doom. This is how we learn that the horrific outcomes we work so hard to prevent were never real and were never going to actually happen.

Surrender is REALLY hard to do the first few times. It requires that you take a leap of faith. In your mind, surrendering to anxiety, panic, and fear is the equivalent to jumping off a very tall building into total darkness. You are sure that death awaits when you jump. But there is a net down there. It will catch you. You will be safe. I promise there is. I, and everyone else who has solved this problem and recovered, has landed in the net. We didn't believe it was there until we actually jumped into it. We were sure there was no net. But there was. It was there to catch us, just as those who came before us assured it would be.

Now it's your turn to trust in the invisible net.

If you surrender to the worst fate you can imagine, you will take that leap off that cliff, and you will land in the net. You will be safe. You will be OK. Then once you know through experience that the net is there; everything begins to change.

Why am I using such vivid, scary imagery here? I am doing that for a reason. I'm not trying to frighten you or scare you away. I want you to understand the process, even if the process isn't what you want it to be. You want it to be a gentler and less scary. You want it to be easier. Sometimes we can get what we want without doing hard stuff. Sometimes we can't. This is one of those times.

I know, it sounds easier to "accept and float." That's what Claire Weekes said, but Dr. Weekes never had the benefit of the internet. She never had 10,000 people tell her that they CAN'T accept and float because those words do not actually match the experience. Accepting sounds too similar to "liking." Trust me, you are not required to like any of this for it to work. Accepting also implies some kind of long-term situation. It scares people into thinking that they must accept feeling afraid forever. "Floating" confuses many because of the positive connotation of the word. Floating is generally a gentle, positive experience. People like to float. It's relaxing. Then they try to "float" through panic and proclaim that it was impossible and that they will never try it again. They expect a to feel calmer just because they are floating, but it NEVER works that way.

Surrender is brutal. It's harsh. But it's accurate. Surrender is short. Surrender isn't complicated. Nobody expects surrender to be a pleasant experience. Surrender is easier to translate into ACTION.

We need to experience hard, scary things. We need to learn through those experiences. And we do that by surrendering to our anxiety and panic, and to the outcomes we have imagined and fear so much.

Then they never happen.

This is why you must resign yourself to surrender. It is the most effective path to the lessons your brain so desperately needs.

Surrender now. Be free later.

It would be ridiculous for me to tell you to surrender without describing what that looks like and how to do it. So if you need to take a break, get composed, or re-read this lesson a few times, do that. Understand what I am saying here.

Then, let's move on to the details of exactly how to surrender.

Lesson 3.2

Do The Opposite

Now that I've hit you over the head with an uncomfortable concept, It's time to get OK with some uncomfortable truth.

Write this down. The solution to this problem lies in doing the opposite of everything you've been doing and think you should do. Before there can be any solution, you must accept this to be true. You must accept that all the fighting, running, avoiding, and seeking safety and comfort has been wrong. None of this has saved you, because you've never needed saving. But all these behaviors have quite likely made things worse for you. Before you can truly move forward, you need to be OK with the idea that it's time to do the opposite of what you've always done.

The single most common mistake I see concerning dealing with anxiety is the misguided idea that the goal is safety and comfort. This is incorrect. The goal is to learn to feel anxiety, fear, and even panic without being afraid of it. You must be afraid for a short time to learn how not to be afraid for a long time. You must experience short-term fear and discomfort before you can achieve long-term comfort. This may sound utterly insane to you. Nobody wants to be afraid or uncomfortable!

Trust me when I tell you that this drive for safety and comfort represents the most significant obstacle on the way to recovery from your anxiety problems. If everything you have been doing up to this point has been geared toward feeling safe and comfortable, then you've been doing it wrong, and that has to change.

It's time to start doing the opposite. Let's take a look at what that looks like.

In the most basic and straightforward form, doing the opposite means doing...NOTHING.

When confronted with high anxiety or panic, you have two choices.

You can do something which you have been doing to no avail, or you can do nothing.

Both will get you to the same place. You will be OK. You will be shaken up, afraid and uncomfortable, but still OK. Doing nothing is faster than doing something. Doing nothing and still being OK teaches your brain the lessons it needs to learn to enact real, lasting change in your life. When the chips are down and you are engulfed in level 10 panic, and when you feel like you can't remember what to do, you can fall back on an easy plan...do nothing.

But nothing is really doing the opposite of everything you've been doing.

If you've been running away, stay put.

If you've been trying to talk yourself down, be silent.

If you've been fidgeting and pacing, be still.

If you've been running to safe people, be alone.

If you've been tensing and bracing, be limp.

If you've been holding your breath, breathe.

The opposite of doing something is doing nothing, so do that. It's about the most manageable plan to remember, and it will slowly change your life for the better. Do nothing. Just be. Do the opposite. I know you have a million questions about how to do this. We'll get to that.

Let's widen this scope. What else is the opposite?

- If you're afraid to drive and you've been avoiding that, start driving.

- If you're afraid to be home alone and you've been finding ways to avoid that, it's time to start being alone.

- If you're afraid to go shopping and you haven't done that in some time, it's time to start shopping again.

- If you'll only leave the house or go far from home with your safe people, it's time to leave them home and start venturing out on your own.

- If you want to cancel your plan to have lunch with a friend, don't cancel. Go.

- If you want to stay in bed and hide under the covers, don't. Get up, take a shower, and get dressed.

- If you want to check your pulse or visit WebMD to see if you're dying, don't. Keep your hands off yourself, throw your phone and/or laptop in the freezer (please don't really do that), and let all your thoughts and sensations be there without reacting to them.

- If you want to complain about how people "don't understand," don't. Take an objective look at yourself and your behaviors. Put yourself in the shoes of others. Try to see how they have a hard time understanding why you're afraid to go to Grandma's birthday party.

- If you want to go online to seek validation and reassurance, don't. Instead, find encouragement and empowerment. Seek inspiration from those that are making progress ahead of you. Seek out success stories and let them show you the way forward.

In a nutshell, every decision you've been making to avoid being afraid and uncomfortable has to be reconsidered and reversed. Take all those things you've been doing, then start doing the opposite.

I'm not talking about going from housebound to a world cruise overnight. We're not going to throw you into the deep water and force you to swim for your life.

That's never how this works.

We will get into the details of this strategy when we create your recovery plan. For now, understand that you will be embarking on a journey to systematically and incrementally do the things that you've been afraid to do and have been avoiding for so long. We will chip away at this avoidance bit by bit. You will rebuild your life bit-by-bit, doing the opposite in a controlled, systematic, and repetitive way. I promise I am not going to tell you to get in your car and drive six hours away from your home by yourself in the middle of the night. Not right away. That would be a bad plan. But you will get to the point where doing that will be no different than walking from one room to another in your home. You will get there by doing the opposite.

Are you still wondering exactly when I lost my mind?

I know this may sound like total nonsense to you. I'm telling you that you are going to intentionally make yourself afraid and uncomfortable—the very state you dread and have been trying so desperately to avoid and eliminate at all costs. Given that it is the opposite of what you've been doing, it's natural to think of it as crazy talk. I assure you it is not.

Remember the 20,000 or so words you read in the first two chapters? The part where we went over bad brain habits and incorrectly learned lessons? Remember how we talked about why avoidance doesn't work given the cognitive model of this problem? Think about all those concepts. Your brain has learned some incorrect lessons and subsequently formed some bad habits. These habits are all based on an erroneous connection between fear and danger. Your job is not to feel safe and comfortable. Your job is to break that incorrect connection and erase those bad cognitive habits. This can't happen through thinking or talking or listening. This happens through experiential learning. This happens through DOING. Specifically, DOING the opposite! So while it might seem like I am talking complete nonsense here, what I am saying is true. Not only is it true, but it is the basis of the most effective treatment we have today for anxiety disorders.

Doing the opposite is the cornerstone of cognitive behavior graduated exposure therapy, and it works. It's not easy. It's not comfortable. It requires that you put in some hard work, but it's damn useful. Millions of people every year overcome this exact problem in this exact way.

Now it's your turn.

Remember when I said that you're not broken or ill?

This is where we put that premise into action. Your brain is a fantastic creation. It's as powerful as it has always been. It's just pointed in the wrong direction. By doing the opposite, we will point it in the right direction and use the exact mechanisms that created this problem to finally solve it.

This will be hard work, so be ready. Doing the opposite of what your body and mind are telling you to do is not an automatic behavior for human beings. This is something you must learn and practice, and you will get better at it with repetition. You may find yourself frustrated and discouraged at times but remember that having proper expectations can help to minimize that. Expect a bumpy road at times so that you won't be surprised when you find yourself in that spot. Learning to do the opposite takes persistence, focus, and a willingness to be TEMPORARILY afraid and uncomfortable. I am going to ask you to be tenacious and disciplined in your approach when we make your recovery plan and talk about how to execute it. Get ready for that, too.

I am going to remind you from time to time that the things most worth accomplishing in life are often difficult. This is one of those times. Before you turn the page, or swipe, or listen to the next section, take a moment and get OK with these ideas. You may be nervous about all this, and that's fine. Just try to find some optimism and hope to go along with those nerves. This is going to be exciting, so let's keep going!

Lesson 3.3

Change Your Focus

Think about the last hour or two of your day. How much of that time did you spend thinking about how you feel?

How much of your attention was spent on the sensations in your body and the thoughts in your head?

I'm willing to wager that it was a considerable amount.

Thinking about how you feel is a significant part of the problem. Changing that is a crucial part of understanding the solution.

When stuck in the anxiety-fear-panic cycle, your focus is almost continually inward. You are focused on every sensation in your body. You are aware of every little change. You are always scanning for the next sensation. You are always preparing for the worst. You notice every tingle, tickle, twitch, pain, and itch. You're aware not only of your overall temperature but the temperature of individual parts of your body. I know I was. You're likely spending an excessive amount of time with your fingers on your neck or wrist—taking your pulse and assessing the speed and consistency of your heartbeat. You're poking, prodding, tugging, massaging, and otherwise manipulating various parts of your body in response to everything you feel. You may be continually testing your ability to take a "deep" breath.

It doesn't stop with the physical sensations. You're living in your head all the time. Every thought becomes a lengthy conversation with yourself about your general condition and level of safety. You feel, and you think. You discuss things with yourself. You debate. You try to reason with your anxious mind.

You lose.

The cycle repeats.

If you are awake, your brain is lit up in a continual cycle of scanning, analyzing, and reacting.

How do I feel now?

How did I feel 20 minutes ago?

Why did it change?

What caused it?

How will I feel in another 20 minutes?

What can I do about all this?

This extreme inward focus is acting as a bottomless can of gasoline, dripping endlessly upon an already roaring fire. It keeps your body on high alert and your brain in high gear. Continuous inward focus is based on irrationality. It fuels fear. It is absolutely exhausting.

Trust me, I know. I was you.

To make matters worse, your inward focus isn't just about what's happening inside your body and mind. That inward focus also acts like a giant magnet, sucking the outside world into the swirling vortex that is your racing brain. Every event is evaluated based on how it makes you feel. It doesn't matter what the event is.

The weather.

A crying child.

An annoying boss.

An angry spouse.

The news.

What you see on Facebook.

What you ate.

What you didn't eat.

The party you've been invited to.

The price of tea in China.

It doesn't matter.

If it's happening in the Universe today, you are likely to quickly internalize it and evaluate it based on how it makes YOU feel.

Is it a trigger?

Was I triggered?

How do I feel now?

Anxiety-based inward focus makes everything about you. This doesn't make you selfish or narcissistic. It's just that in your current state, the world is all about you and how you're feeling.

This is a challenging way to live. It will fuel the cycle we're trying to break. It can lead to discouragement, despair, and a distorted view of yourself as being in worse shape than you really are. Everything from pain in your knee to a cloud passing over the sun is evaluated as a possible anxiety trigger. This can make you feel like you are terrible at life and beyond hope.

Don't worry. That is simply not true.

The odds are very high that at least one person in your life has told you that you "need to get out of your head."

I heard plenty of suggestions. Take a vacation. Sure, that's just what an agoraphobic wants to do.

Go to a movie. Read a book. Listen to music. Go for a walk. "You gotta get out of your head, man!"

At base value, this is true, but it's really not that simple.

I am aware that you really WANT to get out of your own head. I'm sure you try to enjoy the things you used to enjoy, but you may be struggling with this. Conversations, movies, music, and books may be difficult for you to focus on and enjoy because you simply "can't" stay out of the scanning loop. We're going to fix that.

A big part of understanding the solution to this anxiety problem is getting a grip on what this inward focus really is. At its heart, being consumed with how you feel all the time is a safety and avoidance behavior.

These are behavioral and cognitive patterns that you've developed to detect threats and take evasive action when they appear. Threat detection and response are vital to survival, but in your case, that mechanism has gone off the rails. Your brain has built an erroneous link between how you feel, being afraid, and danger. Since how you feel is now interpreted as a threat, your internal safety systems—threat detection and response—are in overdrive. They're working overtime when they really could be chilling on a beach somewhere.

This isn't a matter of only "getting out of your own head." If it were that easy, you'd have done it by now. Actually, you probably have done it, but with limited success. Since it's probably been your primary strategy for dealing with this, let's talk about distraction.

Distraction is a sure-fire way to get out of your own head and to focus on something other than your own body and mind. Distraction works! Temporarily. You likely have built several distraction-based strategies that you turn to when things get dicey. Coloring books, calling someone, snapping rubber bands, splashing cold water on your face, and turning to "comforting" podcasts, videos and music are all common distraction strategies. They often will bring about some relief, but that relief is short-lived. Take away the distraction, and you're right back to scanning for the next threat. Without the distraction, nothing has changed. You've gotten through a rough 30 minutes only to find yourself right back in the thick of it 30 minutes after that. I know how frustrating this can be.

As we go about building a recovery plan in the next chapter, we will leave the distractions behind. Instead, we will focus on your focus. We'll work on actively moving your attention away from every new "threat" to somewhere else, usually your breath. You'll learn to turn AWAY from that firestorm of threats rather than turning toward them to formulate a response. This will seem very wrong at first. Since your brain is convinced that the slight swelling in your ankle will lead to certain death, you will literally be turning your back on what you think is an actual threat to your safety.

But you will learn—through continued practice—that you CAN turn your back on an erroneously perceived threat. This is entirely possible. When you do that, your brain will scream at you to turn back around and engage, but you will not. You will learn to put your focus where YOU want it, not where your mistaken brain craves it.

By the way, if your problem is anxiety centered around your health, the focus I am talking about is the part of the plan that you're going to care about most.

In understanding, embracing, learning, and practicing this skill, you will teach your brain—through repeated experience—that it has been wrong about every one of those threats.

As you retrain your brain this way, you will find that your focus will begin to change. You will slowly regain the ability to engage in the world as a "normal" person. One day you will discover that you've spent 30 minutes just playing with your dog without thinking about how you feel. That will be a wonderful experience, and it will become more frequent as you progress. You can and will break out of your own head, free of the formerly irresistible drive to scan and analyze all the time. Things will change for you.

This, by itself, is not the whole solution. Still, as you regain the ability to think beyond yourself and engage beyond yourself, you will find that your ability to react (or more accurately NOT react) to anxiety and panic will improve. You will be better equipped to intentionally go into those scary situations and do hard things. Changing your focus and breaking that obsession with how you feel will be the engine that drives your overall recovery.

Learning to change your focus from internal to external is going to be vital as we move on to the next concept—

going TOWARD the scary stuff rather than away from it. Get

ready. Sh*t is about to get REAL.

Lesson 3.4

Stop Avoiding:

Going INTO Fear

In lesson 2.6, we talked about why avoiding the things you fear doesn't help you in any way. Rather than solving this problem, avoidance makes it worse.

Remember, avoidance is seeking short term-comfort, but it reinforces long-term suffering.

So, it's time to stop avoiding. It's time to start going toward your fear rather than away from it.

If you've ever heard about exposure therapy, this is it. Intentionally going toward fear is the basis of exposure. In this lesson, we will talk about what it means to go directly toward your anxiety and why this will help you in the long run. If you're already imagining things that you don't want to do this and you're getting nervous at the thought of it, congrats! You just took the first tiny step in the right direction.

Being intentionally afraid and uncomfortable seems like a ridiculous plan, doesn't it? Well, aside from the fact that nobody wants to be frightened and uncomfortable, there's a reason it seems absurd to you. The faulty cognitive link between fear and danger is still trapping you. In your mind, being afraid and being unsafe are the same thing, and you've been acting accordingly.

I would never tell you to do something dangerous, but right now, when you hear me say that you must go toward your fear, you're hearing me telling you to do the unthinkable. You're hearing me urging you to run toward certain death, insanity, embarrassment, or whatever else you fear will happen when you are afraid.

People have gotten furious with me for even suggesting this approach because they filtered my words through their erroneous connection between discomfort and peril.

Some tell me that I am out of my mind.

These are the people who view being afraid as something you should NEVER intentionally do. I might as well be telling them to jump off the nearest 50-story building. They genuinely see it that way.

Do you see it that way?

Being unwilling even to entertain this notion is a function of not accepting the error in cognition that I am describing. If you're ready to bail because the idea of going toward your fear seems unthinkable, I urge you to consider how often you make incorrect judgments daily. We are wrong all the time about all kinds of things. We form opinions that turn out to be incorrect. We pre-judge. We draw faulty conclusions and make bad decisions based on incomplete or wrong information. We think we know something only to see suddenly that we never really did. Being wrong is a universal human function. If you can be wrong about your last boyfriend or girlfriend, why can't you be wrong about being in danger during a panic attack? Think about it.

So why do we have to go toward the fear? Why do this crazy thing? How will this solve your problem? To answer that, we need to look at the mechanism of learning.

Let's think about the ways we learn things:

1. We learn by passive assimilation of information. I tell you how to scramble an egg, and you learn how to do it. You read a book about how to make scrambled eggs, and you incorporate that information into a cognitive model of egg scrambling. But while you

may listen and read, you have still not scrambled that egg.

2. We learn via modeling. You can watch YouTube videos of chefs scrambling eggs. By viewing, you add to your knowledge. Your cognitive model of what it means to scramble an egg grows and gets stronger. This cognitive model is great, but no matter how many videos you watch, that egg is still intact in your refrigerator. You haven't scrambled it yet.

3. We learn by doing. Doing equals experiential learning. You go into the kitchen armed with the knowledge you've gained from reading and watching, and you scramble your first egg. You may make a mistake or two. It may turn out badly, but then you try again, and again. After a few tries, you are enjoying a delicious scrambled egg that you made yourself.

To solve this problem of ours—learning, we need methods 1 and 2, but the real magic is in method 3. Experiential learning.

You will solve your problem by leveraging the amazing ability of your brain to turn a cognitive model into overt behavior and to refine that behavior through repetition.

We go toward the fear because we must learn through experience that while you are afraid and uncomfortable, you are not actually in danger. We do this to break that erroneous fear/danger connection that fuels your anxiety problem and keeps you stuck.

No amount of talking about it, reading about it, hearing explanations, or watching videos of people doing it will break that connection. Only DOING—learning through experience—will break it and set you free.

Sadly, this is where many people stumble. They spend a tremendous amount of time thinking about this. They read. They learn. They discuss. They, however, remain unwilling to actually DO. Thinking, learning, reading, and talking is part of this process, but *only the doing* will matter, so you have to be OK with that idea.

You must start from these premises:

1. A mistaken link between fear and danger fuels your intense desire NOT to do this.

2. While you hate going toward your worst fears, you are not actually in any danger. You must trust that you are safe even though your brain is SCREAMING at you that you are not.

3. By doing this hard thing in the PROPER way (we'll get to that soon), you will break the mistaken link, and you will learn how NOT to be afraid of how you feel when anxious or in a state of panic.

If you're good with hanging your hat on these three premises, let's continue. Let us get a deeper understanding of what going toward the fear is all about.

Here's a hint: it's never the thing or the place. It's always how you feel while doing the thing or going to the place. This is critical. If you are afraid of being in the supermarket, it is not about the supermarket at all. The supermarket is irrelevant in this equation. Your fear of the supermarket is the same fear that makes you afraid to be alone, makes you find all the hospitals around you at all times, and makes you check your pulse 200 times in a typical day. If you fear the drive-through at McDonald's because it makes you feel trapped, then you also fear driving on the highway because you can't just get off any time you want to. You fear getting involved in a conversation with an old friend after church for the same reason. McDonald's, the highway, and the friend waiting to start a conversation are all the same thing. Attack one, and you attack them all.

When we talk about going toward the fear, we talk about the fear itself, regardless of where or why it appears. If you want to be able to go to Disneyland with your family, you must learn to stand and have a conversation with your old friend after church because it's the same fear. You fear how you feel because you've linked it to danger. In the end, it's always that, so we will attack the fear, not the specific tasks or destinations.

I don't care about those.

I only care about the experience of passing through fear and discomfort in the most constructive, non-reactive, non-avoidant way. If that's in the supermarket, great. If it's in your front yard, great. If it's in an airport, that's fine, too. It doesn't matter.

I need you to remember this. Too many people get stuck, thinking that each task or goal is unique. They are not. If you understand the mechanism at play, you will have a much easier time moving from goal to goal without having to re-think and "prepare" each time you do so.

After starting this journey, people often say that they're making great strides, only to stop and ask how to tackle something new.

The answer is always the same. If you've managed to get good at the supermarket, tackling your dentist appointment next month is based on the same exact mechanism and will involve the same approach. So, you won't have to continually ask how to do the next item on your goals list. Because you'll already know from having done the first few things.

Ultimately, going toward fear means:

1. Putting the brakes on your old avoidance and retreat routines. Those must be left behind.

2. Identifying the tasks, places, and situations that make you feel anxious or trigger panic.

3. Identifying your current safety rituals and behaviors so you can be prepared to drop them while going toward fear.

4. Going toward these tasks, places, and situations without engaging in those fear-driven safety behaviors and rituals. You have to learn to do these things without going into freak out mode. This is the "secret sauce" that makes the entire recipe work. We will talk about this in the next lessons.

5. Learning how to tell the proper story about your ventures into fear and discomfort. Constructively describing those experiences—telling stories that focus on actual positive outcomes rather than the imagined "almost happened disasters"—is part of the solution to this problem.

As with many of these lessons, I'm going to ask you to take a little time to think about this. Wrap your brain around what lies ahead and what you need to do. Ask yourself if you're ready to intentionally put yourself into the situations you've been avoiding for so long. It will be unpleasant and difficult at first. There's no way around that. It will get easier over time, though. I promise.

As you think about this, keep one important thing in mind. You will never be fully "ready" to do this. You will be afraid. You won't want to do it. That's the way it's supposed to be. That's why this works. Do not make the mistake of thinking that you must learn how not to be afraid before you start this process. You can't learn how not to be afraid until you do what we're going to discuss. Only through the doing—the being afraid—can you lose that fear. So, get yourself ready for a leap of faith that this process will work.

First, you will leap, then you will learn. Not the other way around.

Now, let's talk about that "secret sauce" I mentioned and look at the concept of understanding and changing your reaction to fear and discomfort. It's where the learning will happen. Ready?

Lesson 3.5

Examining Your Reactions

We've arrived.

These lessons are where all the magic really happens. Everything else we talk about, and everything else I say, is meaningless if you don't first get on board with having to change your reaction to anxiety. Then you must learn how to do it. This is the part where your brain learns that It's been wrong and that you don't have to be afraid of how you feel and what you think.

Let's get started.

It's never about how you feel. Never. NEVER. It's always about how you REACT to how you feel. Always. Never the feeling, always the reaction. I cannot say this enough. It's never the feeling. It's always the reaction. The feelings and the thoughts are most certainly real, scary, and uncomfortable, but that doesn't matter. It's how you REACT to those sensations and thoughts that wire your brain one way or the other. Let me explain.

There are three reactions that we have to understand and address.

The Reaction Before

This is the realm of anticipation and anticipatory anxiety. You are faced with a task or situation that you fear. You react to that fear in an extreme way. This causes you to prepare for a 20-minute drive down the highway in the same way you would prepare to swim the English Channel in a hurricane surrounded by angry sharks.

I'm going to use a drive on the highway as an example. The concept applies across multiple situations and tasks. Please keep this in mind.

The minute you knew you'd be driving on the highway—doing something you usually avoid out of fear—you become entirely focused on the upcoming challenge. You think about it, and think about it, and think about it. Do any of these thoughts sound familiar?

- *How will I ever do this?*
- *What if I panic? How will I manage?*
- *Who can come with me? Will I be driving near people that can help if I need it?*

- *Can I cancel?*
- *I don't want to do this!*
- *I can't do this!*

You visualize the worst case and plan your escape and rescue. You re-live past bad experiences in your mind. You engage in a running debate with your brain. This could wind up being horrible, but you know you have to do it anyway. Once in a while, you manage to forget about it and calm down. Then you remember, and it all kicks into high gear again. Sometimes you experience a wave of courage and resolve. You declare that you are going to do this once and for all! Ten minutes later, your courage is gone, and you're afraid and unsure again.

You make a plan, but your plan centers around what you can do to survive that upcoming 20-minute drive. *What do I need to bring? I have to make sure my phone is charged! Are there any hospitals along the route? Are there lots of shops and houses along the way? Is it isolated? How long are the stretches between exits? Maybe I should bring some snacks and an extra bottle of water? I better check twice to be sure*

I have my Xanax before I leave. If I get there but think I can't make the drive home, can I call an Uber and get my car later?

You pace.

You try to breathe to calm down now and then.

You ask your anxiety friends for tips on how to handle it.

You think about EVERYTHING, but the moment you are currently in. You're entirely future-focused with an emphasis on protecting yourself against disaster.

You prepare for your 20-minute drive down the highway like you would prepare for a tightrope walk across the Grand Canyon. This level of dread and preparation would also hold true for an upcoming social engagement, knowing you will be home alone tomorrow, or the annual Christmas concert at your child's school. The exact driving related items won't apply, but you are aware of how you prepare for those other things, too. I know you are.

And I know that you are preparing for the worst experience of your life...all the time.

When you react this way, when you prepare this way, you are teaching your brain that you are about to walk through Hell and that your safety and security is in question. You are conditioning yourself to equate the upcoming event with an actual threat. Does this sound like a good "before" reaction?

The Reaction During

This is what you do when anxious or heading toward panic. When you experience a sensation or thought that you associate with danger, you tense. You go into bracing and fighting mode. You look for escape and exit options. You distract yourself. You turn to "rescuers" to save you from your fear, discomfort, and the horrible fate you believe you are heading toward. You launch into your carefully developed and curated sequence of safety behaviors. You react to how you feel and what you think the same way you would respond to being held at gunpoint or your house being on fire.

Back to our highway drive example. This may all sound familiar. You've started on shaky ground to begin with.

Why?

Because you associate this situation with fear and discomfort, and you've incorrectly associated fear and discomfort with danger. You try to convince yourself over and over and over that you are OK. It's only 20 minutes. I can do this! You scan continuously for any sign of the monster.

How am I feeling now? Uh-oh. Did my heart just skip a beat? How am I breathing? Am I doing this correctly? How much longer? Still 18 minutes?!?!?!?!

At the first sign of a feared sensation or powerful negative thought, you go into bracing/fighting mode. You tense your muscles and grip the wheel even tighter, trying to prove to yourself that you're still holding it and in control.

You hold your breath.

You crank up the air conditioner and blast it in your face.

Maybe It's the dead of winter, and you open the car window to get that blast of cold air.

You go for your bottle of water.

You pop a mint into your mouth.

You turn up the radio and try to sing along.

You think about 74 different people that you want to call.

You know you shouldn't, but you keep thinking that you should.

Your eyes are peeled for the next exit—looking for your escape hatch.

You wiggle in your seat as the panic rises.

You look around for rescue points—a shop you can run into, a firehouse, a hospital, or doctor's office.

You pick up your phone, then put it down, then pick it up, then put it down.

All the while, you're arguing with your brain, trying to convince yourself that you're OK. Every logical thought you have is countered by "what if?", so you argue harder with yourself. You declare—maybe out loud—that you hate this.

You need to get home!

You white-knuckle your way to a highway exit.

You try to remember which direction home is.

You head in that direction.

You curse every stop sign and red light.

You hate every slow car on the road.

You're keep trying to convince yourself you're OK.

You're still eyeing your phone to make that rescue call as you look around for rescue points.

You're trying to take REALLY deep breaths because that will calm you down, right?

As you get closer to home, you start to feel better. Your heart is slowing down. The fear isn't as intense. Your brain is quieting down. The argument is getting easier to win. You're going to be OK. You're shaky, but you think you're going to make it. You start to relax. Just two more minutes, and you've made it.

Let's review your trip.

You started by scanning for trouble, then continued by reacting to thoughts and sensations as if your life was in danger. Everything you did and everything you thought while you were in the midst of panic was an attempt to protect yourself against certain doom. Your reaction was based on fighting, bracing, and escaping. Your response affirmed to your brain that you *must* fight, brace, and escape. You reinforced the belief that being afraid and uncomfortable is something that you must avoid at all costs. You've had this reaction for weeks. Or months. Or years. Given where you are now, reading these words, do you think that reaction has been serving you well?

The Reaction After

This is the reaction most people forget about, but It's just as important as the other two. Maybe even more critical in certain situations. Your reaction after bad experiences is all about storytelling. You recount the event using words like "horrible," "awful," and "terrifying." You describe the incident as if you really did narrowly escape death, insanity, or some other horrible fate. You seek out others who have had similar experiences so you can share in the horribleness of it all and not feel alone.

Back to our example.

When you get home, you turn off the car and breathe a heavy sigh. You're still very shaky and feeling unstable and vulnerable. You feel better than you did, but you're afraid that it could all get triggered again at any moment.

You slowly walk yourself into your house and go to a comfortable spot. You're so thankful that you "made it." You're home now, so you're starting to calm down even more. You're starting to worry less about a possible next wave. Thank God you didn't lose control! Good thing it happened before you got too far down the highway! Luckily there wasn't too much traffic, so you were able to get home pretty quickly. You may get yourself a drink or something to eat. When you calm down enough, you may go online and tell everyone in your anxiety support groups what just happened. Every time you tell the story, you tell it as if you have just miraculously survived a 40-story fall from a tall building.

Your reaction after the fact, i.e., the way that you tell the story, has reinforced the connection between fear and danger. The story you are telling yourself and the rest of the world is a story of courageous survival in the face of an inevitable disaster. You are teaching yourself that you "made it" only because of *what* you did. The bracing. The fighting. The fleeing. The running home. Your story asserts these were all necessary reactions that enabled you to be saved.

Has your reaction after the fact—the story you tell— served you well? Has it helped you find a better way, or has it kept you stuck in this spot, still unsure of the way out?

I GET IT!

Now What?

So It's not the sensations and the thoughts. It never is. It's always the reaction that matters. Now that we've seen how your responses are wiring your brain to equate anxiety with danger, what can we do about it?

Well, we can learn to change those reactions. We can learn to eliminate them. We can learn to quite literally do NOTHING in the face of anxiety and panic.

That's it. That's the magic right there. If you made it this far, congrats. You now know the secret to recovery. You're welcome. :-)

All joking aside, I want you to consider how awesomely simple this concept is. Change the way you react to your anxiety. Learn to do...nothing. There are no tests and medical procedures to undergo. No special foods to eat or drink. No herbs or supplements to mess with. No medication to adjust. No spiritual journey to go on. Just learn to do....NOTHING. The plan is brilliant in its simplicity.

But there's one small detail to remember: simple doesn't equal easy.

Meaning it's a simple concept, but difficult to put into play. It's difficult because it requires you to do the exact opposite of what you've been doing and what you want to do. It requires you to go toward the fear rather than away from it. It requires you to be courageous, persistent, and tenacious. That's hard work!

Hard doesn't equal impossible, though.

Let's take a look at what it means to change your reaction.

Lesson 3.6

Changing Your Reactions

We've seen the three reactions that are driving that faulty brain link between fear and danger. The reaction before, the reaction during, and the reaction after. Now that we understand how they work; we can look at how to change them into something more straightforward and more effective. All by doing NOTHING.

You heard me. NOTHING. We're going take all the "something" that you've been doing to save yourself and turn it into "nothing." We are going to prevent all those old reactions and replace them with no response. Why? Because "nothing" works, and it works faster and more efficiently than "something."

Exposure therapy is a cornerstone of cognitive-behavioral therapy. But it's not just exposure. It's called EXPOSURE AND RESPONSE PREVENTION (ERP). It's not just about intentionally doing scary things; it's about doing them without responding in the old non-productive ways!

The goal is to teach your brain through experience that it has been wrong all this time. We need to correct the bad lessons your mind has learned and break the bad habits it's developed over time. The way to do this is not to tell it to change or to think about how to change it. The way to do this is to SHOW your brain a new way. The part of your brain responsible for all this doesn't respond to thought, reason, and logic anyway. It must be taught through direct experience.

The experience we need to have to break those lousy brain habits is essentially this:

I experienced anxiety or panic.

I was very afraid.

I was very uncomfortable.

I did NOTHING about it.

I was OK anyway because afraid and uncomfortable do not equal danger.

That's it. Simple lesson. When you feel anxiety and panic, do nothing, and still wind up OK. This is how you teach your brain that all that "stuff" you've been doing has been unnecessary because it's been *wrong* all this time. You've always been OK. Even feeling your worst, you have been OK.

It's not just the exposure. It's the response prevention too!.
This is the cornerstone of EVERYTHING.

This is how you learn to recover.

Right here.

So let's go.

Changing the Reaction Before

When you know you have to do something that you hate to do because you fear it, the first order of business is to accept that you are going to be afraid beforehand. That's how it's going to work. You will be nervous about doing hard and scary things. Welcome to being human.

Expect it. Don't fight it. Let yourself be nervous, but there's no reason to be passive about it. Changing your "before" reaction is about learning to live in the moment you are in, not living in a scary future. Your new "before reaction" is about living your normal life in slow, deliberate, tiny chunks.

Living in the moment is a focus exercise. Imagine you are trying to improve your posture. Each time you find yourself slouching or hunching over, you consciously correct your posture. You stand up straight. You may have to do this over and over throughout the day. Breaking the slouching habit, building the standing up straight habit, takes awareness, action, and repetition. The same goes for learning to change your focus from the future to the present.

In the last lesson, we used a drive on the highway as our example event. Let's continue with that. Remember that the concepts apply across all situations, not just driving.

When you know you are going to be driving on the highway, you will get anxious about it. This is normal. There's no need to try to banish the fear or drown it out. However, when you find yourself thinking about the drive, stop, and return your focus to the present moment. Focus on what you are doing right now. The drive doesn't exist yet. The future hasn't arrived yet. There's absolutely no reason to live it before it does.

Thinking about it, worrying about it, and ruminating about it will not change any outcomes. They will not protect you or save you from any horrible fate. These actions will simply fuel the fear cycle and make anticipatory anxiety even worse. Are you driving right now, or are you reading a book? Are you in the car right now, or are you chewing the eggs you cooked for breakfast? Are you on the highway right now, or are you brushing your teeth? Are you behind the wheel, or are you playing with your dog? Each time your mind goes back to the upcoming event, stop and return it to the present and the activity you are currently engaged in, regardless of what that activity is.

You will find that you have to do this again and again and again. It will be very difficult at first. You may find that you are frustrated. You may think that you have no control over the process.

But you do have control. Like any new skill, this will take time to learn and master. Be patient. This new tactic is not designed to instantly change everything for you. It is designed to change your reaction to fear incrementally over time. That's how this works, so be prepared for that.

When you become aware that you have a difficult and scary event coming up, make a plan, then execute it step by step. The plan is designed to keep you living in the present rather than in the future. It will look something like this:

Every day before the event:

Do not think about the event. When you think about the event, stop. Think about what you're doing in the present. Take each activity you will engage in throughout your days and break them into tiny pieces. Putting groceries away? Don't put them all away at once. Attack every single item as its own project. Focus on each one fully. Pick it up, walk to where it belongs, open the cabinet door, place the item inside, close the cabinet door. Go back for the next item that needs to be put away.

Are you thinking about the drive that will happen in four days? Stop. Return your focus to the box of cereal in your hand and complete the task in progress.

Break everything you are doing into the smallest possible chunks and focus on completing each chunk before moving on to the next.

This likely sounds odd to you. That's OK if it does.

Breaking the act of making tea into 472 discrete steps isn't something you normally do, so it will take some getting used to.

Just do it, even when it feels strange. It will become familiar pretty quickly.

Your goal is to remain in the present and to slow things down. There's no need to rush through your day. Go slow, be deliberate and purposeful in your actions, and remember to keep your body relaxed and your breath flowing.

The day of the event:

Plan every activity leading up to that scary event, then execute that plan. Perform every activity slowly, deliberately, and mindfully.

Start with opening your eyes in the morning, then sitting up, then putting your feet on the floor. Move on to standing up, then walking to the bathroom. Make every step you take before the event drive count. Time to brush your teeth? Just pick up your toothbrush. Then pick up the toothpaste. Then put the toothpaste on the brush. Then put down the toothpaste. Then put the brush in your mouth. Then brush.

Break it all down into that kind of detail and execute every motion intently and with full focus.

Be slow.

Breathe.

Relax your body.

You have no need to live the scary event yet. You still have to shower, get dressed, eat, get the kids off to school, and walk the dog first! As they happen—slowly and mindfully in the sequence—those actions are the only real things. The scary event isn't real yet. It doesn't exist until it does, so getting to that point in this mindful, quiet, slow, focused manner is essential.

Why should you work on living in the moment, slowing down, and breaking your day into tiny slices? What does this have to do with changing your reaction to anxiety and panic?

It has EVERYTHING to do with it.

By taking control of the process and executing a plan, you are forcing your brain to do none of the things it used to do before that scary event. It will not race; it will not obsess; it will not create worst-case scenarios. It will not drag you around, and it will not pour continuous buckets of irrational thoughts and fears over your head. You will be taking that away from your brain. This is important because you will ultimately arrive at the moment where the drive on the highway (for example) begins, but now you will get there without having been on high alert for hours or days beforehand. The lesson you will teach your brain is that it was OK to not go into alert/defend/escape mode. Even remaining quiet, slow and calm got you to the event.

Look, brain! None of that stuff was required. We're still here. Nervous, afraid, and uncomfortable about the drive, but still OK. Now let's go!

Do you see how changing how you react to that "before fear" can teach your brain new lessons? Blocking the old brain habits and still being OK (ready for the highway drive) shows your brain that it doesn't have to do all that stuff any longer. Will your mind learn this lesson immediately? It will not.

This will take repetition and practice. It's a process. Be patient with yourself and stick to the plan. Over time you will teach your brain to approach upcoming "challenges" in a totally different way that doesn't involve being consumed by fear, worry, and dread for hours or days on end.

As with everything we're talking about, doing this is not a shield against anxiety. As you work on living slowly and mindfully and on refocusing your thoughts from the future to the present, you will feel anxious and even afraid. This will be especially true when you first start out. Expect this. You will have to do this work while anxious at first. Do not expect that focusing on your shoelaces will instantly wipe away those feelings. It will not, at least not immediately.

Do this often enough, however, and you will find your anticipatory anxiety is decreasing and that you can actually experience increasing levels of calm even when you have a challenge on the horizon!

Trust the process.

Execute the plan.

Show your brain new things and allow it to learn. You will be amazed at how it will change if you give it a chance.

Changing the Reaction During

This is where the rubber meets the road (no pun intended). Now it's time to actually do that drive on the highway that you've been fearing and avoiding for so long. The difference is that now we're going to do it differently. We're going to allow the fear and discomfort to come without trying to wipe it away or escape from it. This time when those sensations and thoughts arrive, we will do...nothing.

To start, you need to be OK with the fact that you are going to be afraid. Maybe even terrified.

This is to be expected, especially the first few times you try this new approach and intentionally put yourself into anxiety or panic-inducing situations. You will be afraid and uncomfortable, and you may even panic.

Expect it.

Be OK with it.

Understand that experiencing these things with your new "do nothing" plan is how you will teach your brain that it's been wrong all this time!

When you are on that highway and driving along, when you feel your anxiety rising (maybe you even started the drive at near panic levels), the overall strategy is to stop trying to protect yourself against it. Protecting yourself against anxiety and panic hasn't helped you, so we need to stop doing that.

But how?

How do we let our feelings and thoughts surround and engulf us without reacting?

That sounds impossible!

I promise it's not. It's very difficult because it requires that you display courage—even extreme courage—to start. It requires that you make a commitment to trust the process and see it through. You will be taking a leap of faith when you do this. I acknowledge that. Your brain is convinced that you are in real danger, so by deciding to intentionally do scary things AND to do nothing when the alarms start ringing, you are effectively choosing certain doom. *You're not really, but your brain thinks you are, so it will SCREAM at you when you relax and breathe instead of running for help.*

As far as the fear center in your brain is concerned, you may as well be standing still as a speeding train heads directly toward you. The fear will be that intense. This is what makes this a difficult thing to do, especially the first few times. Remember, though, that there really is no speeding train. It's an illusion. Your brain has been mistaken. It's created a danger where none exists. You have to show it that the threat doesn't exist. The only way to do that is to allow the worst possible thing to happen.

Here's the secret: it will not. I promise it won't.

I am not writing a book about how to do dangerous things.

I'm writing a book about how to do hard things. Know and trust the difference.

Let's go back to the car.

Our drive down the highway. How should you react differently? What are the nuts and bolts? Well, there aren't many. This is good news.

Here's how it works.

When you feel a scary sensation in your body, you will want to tense up and brace against it. You will want to fidget and wiggle in your seat. You may want to literally grab yourself. You may want to grab your phone to call for help, or turn up the radio, blast the air conditioning, or open a window. *Do none of these things*. Instead, simply relax your body like a rag doll. Release every bit of tension. Just let it go. In the case of our drive down the highway, keep your hands on the wheel (but no "death grip"), be still in the seat, relax against the seatback, chin up, eyes open. R-E-L-A-X into the fear. Let it wash over you thoroughly. Let it engulf you. Do nothing when it does. Just maintain your position in a relaxed way. This is the exact opposite of what your body and brain are telling you to do. Remember, your brain thinks this is actual danger. It will want you to do something to save yourself.

Don't.

Relax.

Let the tension out of your body.

Drive the car as if you don't have a care in the world. Relax and drive while the fear of the fear tries to kill you, make you insane, or whatever it is you fear will happen. It won't. Those things have never happened, and nothing you have ever done has stopped them from happening. That's because they were NEVER going to happen to begin with. So do nothing with your body except go limp and drive.

Let's talk about your breath. While you are going totally limp, you will breathe. You know all the thousands of times you've heard someone say, "Take a deep breath?" FORGET THAT. You don't need to take a deep breath to calm down. Get that out of your head. No deep breathing, cleansing breaths, or grounding breaths. None of that is needed. All you need is plain old regular breathing. Your body knows exactly how much air to take in, and how much to exhale. It knows when to do this and how to do this. You couldn't stop it if you tried.

You will simply breathe. Breathe through your nose. Breathe into your belly, NOT into your chest. Your shoulders and chest should not be rising and falling with each breath. Your stomach should be expanding and contracting. You will inhale, pause for a brief moment, then exhale for a bit longer than the inhale. Some people like to count. In for four, hold, out for six. You will not attempt to fill your lungs with air. That's chest breathing. You will not sigh on the exhale. This is often done in an attempt to "calm down," but the heavy sigh is a fast, high-volume exhale. This can lead to over-breathing, which can lead to hyperventilation.

If your face, hands, and feet get tingly, you are hyperventilating. If your hands and feet cramp up and lock so you can't use them, you are hyperventilating. I have some useful instruction and links to tutorials on breathing on my website at:

https://theanxioustruth.com/skills.

Learning this and practicing proper breathing all the time when NOT in a panic will help make it the default state when you need it to be.

Now let's look at your thoughts. When you are in a high anxiety or panic state, your brain will lock into high gear. It will scream scary things at you. They will all start with *oh my God or What if?* It will tell you that you are going to die, lose your mind, or look like a fool. Your brain will take your worst fear and yell it in your face at high volume, trying to get you to take evasive action.

This is to be expected.

This is your brain doing what it thinks is its job. It's trying to keep you alive and safe. It doesn't know that you are going to be just fine. It thinks it needs to intervene. When those thoughts are racing through your head and screaming loudly at you, you will NOT answer them.

No self-talk.

No affirmations.

No "talking yourself down."

None of that.

You can't reason with irrational fear. It will never listen to you. There will always be one more *"what if"* thought. Always. Trying to soothe yourself by repeating "I'm OK" is a dead end. It doesn't really work. It's actually counterproductive. Remember, the fear center in your brain isn't listening. And it doesn't learn that way. Trying to counter such thoughts while in a state of panic is like trying to call someone who has their phone turned off. It's impossible.

Instead, while your brain is screaming for your attention, you are going to place your focus elsewhere. You are going to deny its request for attention. Place your focus on the tip of your nose? Why? Because this is where your breath enters and leaves your body, so it's a handy target.

There's no spiritual significance to the tip of your nose or your breath. It's just a convenient focal point. You will breathe like we just talked about breathing, then you will simply bring your focus to the tip of your nose and your breath. When your brain yells, "Oh my God, I'm dying!" you will gently bring your focus to the tip of your nose and your breath.

Let it scream.

Let the thought be there.

Don't try to stop it or argue with it.

When the next thought grabs your attention, you will not respond or engage. You will bring your focus back to the tip of your nose and your breath. You will do this again and again and again and again. It's not easy. You are choosing to dismiss deeply ingrained alarms designed to keep you safe. You are essentially doing the opposite of what you've been programmed to do. Remember that you're not trying to get the scary thoughts and suggestions to stop. You're merely working on letting them be there without engaging with them in any way.

I like to use the tip of my nose and my breath as a focal point, but I also mentally visualize slightly turning my back on my thoughts. Imagine someone coming up to you on the street and screaming in your face. Rather than screaming back, you relax and gently turn you back on the screamer. They may come around to your face again. Relax, and turn your back again. And again. And again. As often as it takes. At some point, your screaming friend will learn that it's pointless, and they will stop screaming. This is what we're doing with our brain and our thoughts. We are trusting that there really is no danger, and never has been, and we are teaching our minds the proper lesson.

Let's go back to our driving scenario once more.

You may have to pull over. That is perfectly acceptable, especially in the early stages of this new approach. You may find that when anxiety and panic arrive that you have to stop what you are doing and actively do this new "nothing."

That is quite common.

Doing nothing is a new skill for you, and you may need to stop everything to focus on being non-reactive to your thoughts and sensations. When driving, this may mean pulling over to the side of the road for a few minutes. This is not wrong or incorrect in any way. The more times you do this, the more you will develop the ability to do nothing while doing other things. I can have a full-blown panic attack while driving, lifting weights in the gym, or having a business meeting.

I am able to do nothing while doing something, but this is the result of years of practice and experience. You will get there, too.

For now, pull over or otherwise stop what you're doing if you need to. That's OK.

When you do nothing during periods of high anxiety and panic, the intense sensations and fear will pass. When you do it well, they will pass much more quickly than you can imagine. When they pass, you will calm down, be less afraid, and will generally feel better. <u>You will have done nothing to save yourself or escape, yet you will feel better faster</u>. You will experience the full force of anxiety, fear, discomfort, and panic, do nothing in response, and wind up perfectly OK.

Can you see how this will teach your brain that there is no need to go into alert mode anymore? This outcome—being OK even after taking no protective or evasive action—is the experience we need to have to break that faulty brain link between fear, discomfort, and danger. Every time you have this experience, that link gets a bit weaker. Over time and with repetition, the link will break. When it does, you will lose your fear of anxiety and panic. When you are no longer afraid of anxiety and panic, EVERYTHING changes. It will be wonderful.

Doing nothing is extremely powerful. Doing nothing leverages the incredible power of your brain to learn and adapt. Doing nothing uses the same mechanism that got you into this mess to get you back out!

Changing The Reaction After

Congrats. You lived the hours or days preceding that scary event differently. You did the event differently. You've learned to be mindful, live in the present, focus where you want to focus, relax, and become non-reactive to the sensations and thoughts that come with anxiety and panic.

Amazing.

Now we need to turn our attention to changing your reaction after the fact. To finish up with our highway driving example, what should you do once the drive is over? You're done. You did it. You're back home, but your work isn't finished yet.

First, recognize the victory! You were afraid beforehand. You were terrified during. You were in a total panic on that highway. That isn't defeat or failure. Remember that you only learn by experiencing these things, so do not look at the experience as bad or negative because you felt fear and discomfort. Understand that you felt fear and discomfort more constructively than you used to. You took a step forward! Even if you weren't able to entirely do nothing and you bailed out halfway through, you still made a step ahead. You took the first steps toward changing your reaction to anxiety and panic. You started to teach your brain new lessons. That's progress! If you made the whole drive and managed to be non-reactive the entire time, that's a bonus. It probably means you've had some practice, and you're getting better at it.

ALWAYS think about what you did better than you used to do. You took a different approach. You did different things. Every change matters. They all add up. From this moment on, feeling poorly isn't a failure. It's not defeat. It's not negative. It's learning.

Next, we need to change the words we use. You didn't "make it."

NEVER say you "made it."

It's inaccurate because you were always going to make it. That was never a question in terms of objective reality. The doubt was false doubt that existed only in your thoughts. Don't give the doubt any more power. You didn't make it. You DID it! Maybe you did it uncomfortably, but you did it. Always say you did it. Remember when you refused to do it? But now, you did it!

Progress!

Stop using inflammatory words and phrases. You were not "in Hell." It wasn't "horrific." You didn't "almost die or pass out." Those phrases and phrases like them have to be removed from your vocabulary. They have never served you well. They are not descriptions of reality. From now on, we only deal in fact, not in your interpretation or feelings.

Next, you will shorten the story. No more long-winded recounting of every scary sensation and thought. They don't need to be described. They only matter in your own head. The story isn't about your rapid heartbeat or depersonalization anymore. That story is part of your problem, so it's time to stop telling it. From now on, your accounts will be objective and concise.

"I drove on the highway for 20 minutes today. It's the first time I've done that in eight months. It was really scary and hard to do, but I did it. I was afraid and uncomfortable, but I was OK. I did it, and I was OK."

See how that story sounds VERY different than the one you've been telling? It's accurate, and it helps to change the way you view things. In the old story, you are being kicked around by anxiety and panic. In the new account, you are in control. Your brain needs to hear that!

Now it's time to think about who gets to hear your new story. YOU have to listen to it without a doubt. It's essential to tell yourself the new story! Who else should you tell? You may choose to keep it to yourself. That's perfectly fine. I generally did my work in silence without sharing much of it with anyone else. That was my way. If that's your way, great. If not, that's great, too. Just be careful about who you share your new story with.

What reaction are you getting? Are you getting encouragement to keep going? Are you getting support? Are you telling your new story to cheerleaders, or are you telling your new story to people who will dismiss it, minimize it, and immediately make it about themselves and why they can't or won't follow suit?

This can be a problem, especially online. Do your best to surround yourself with people who will be happy when they hear your new story. Look for people who will encourage you to keep going. Seek out people who may share your struggle but will use your new story to motivate and inspire them.

This matters.

Finally, and most importantly, instead of being happy that you're back to your safe zone, plan to do that hard thing again right away. Or a different hard thing. Gone are the days where you brute force and white-knuckle your way through the supermarket only to "reward" yourself with four days at home afterward. Supermarket in the morning, walk around the block in the afternoon. Then do it again tomorrow. Stop reacting to these events like you've earned a vacation afterward.

There are no vacations in recovery. Celebrate the progress and plan for more.

Look forward to it. Doing these things is proactive. You're actively engaging in the process of recovery. Talk about it and plan for it accordingly!

When you change your "after" reaction you change how you tell the story and who you tell it to. You change your next steps from retreat to repetition. Doing these things teaches your brain the new lessons it needs to learn.

When we change our reactions to anxiety, panic, and fear before, during, and after episodes of high anxiety or panic, we set our brains on a new path. We weaken incorrect links and build new productive and positive connections. We leave wrong answers and bad cognitive habits behind while learning proper lessons and developing good brain habits.

Changing our reactions is a simple idea yet challenging to put into practice. When you find your courage, get determined, and do the work, you will learn it will be well worth it.

Then the day will come—maybe sooner than you think—when you suddenly find yourself not gripped by fear and worry all the time. That will be a great day. I promise it will.

Lesson 3.7

Learning New Skills

Solving your anxiety problem requires that you learn some new skills and practice them religiously. We know now that the key to recovery lies in changing how we react to anxiety and fear. Let's take a look at some skills that you'll want to start working on. Learning these things and practicing them religiously will be a huge help in changing direction and moving down the path toward a new life.

Before I start, it's important for me to clarify one important thing. The skills I am going to tell you about are NOT shields against panic or anxiety. Do not look at them as such. They are not designed to prevent panic or stop it dead in its tracks. When panic arrives, do not expect that breathing will end it immediately. These are not prevention or escape measures. These are tools that you will use to maintain a state of non-reaction, even at the height of panic. Remaining physically relaxed and mentally calm while anxiety and panic rage around you will help it all to end sooner, but it will not make it all end immediately. This is critically important for you understand and accept before moving ahead. I've seen too many people experience panic, try to stop it dead in its tracks with breathing techniques, then call it failure because that "didn't work." That's not how this works, so please be realistic in your expectations.

Our goal is to learn to remain still and non-reactive in the face of anxiety and panic, not to prevent it from happening or to squash it dead when it does. I can't stay this often enough.

Additionally, it's vitally important to remember that this is a learning process. I'm often confronted by people who get upset when they use the skills we're going to talk about but still "feel afraid" or "still panic." That is exactly what is going to happen. I'm not going to teach you how to not panic. That's not ever the goal here.

I'm trying to teach you how to be anxious and how to panic without going into high alert freak out mode. Experiencing anxiety or even panic is never the problem. What you do when it happens defines the problem. Don't ask why you had a panic attack "even though I'm relaxing and breathing." Instead, examine what you did when panic arrived. That's all you care about in this process.

Relaxing the Body, Slowing Down

Let's start with staying physically relaxed. I've heard it said many times that our physical behavior sends signals to the fear center in our brains. When you go into a tensed, braced, high energy physical state, you are sending very clear "fight or flight" signals to your brain.

It would be preferable to go into a relaxed, non-resisting, low-energy physical state. This is difficult and takes practice; however, it is quite possible to learn and to master. Putting yourself into a physically relaxed state when anxiety rises tells your brain that the need to fight or flee has passed and that a state of high alert is not required.

I need to clarify what "physically relaxed" and "low energy" mean. When you are in a state of high anxiety, your body will naturally react in certain automatic ways. Your heartbeat and your breath will become more rapid. Adrenaline will do this to you. It will also make you feel "amped up," nervous and on edge. It will make you feel like you want to move, or that you are unable to sit still.

Expect this.

I know this sounds like the opposite of relaxation, but trust me, it is still possible to put the controllable parts of your body into a relaxed, low energy state even when the automatic parts are not. When you go limp and relax as much as you can, you are creating a state where adrenaline can do its job, then dissipate naturally. You are helping to prevent a "second wave" of fear. You are also showing your brain that it is possible to not fight the panic and the fear, and still be OK. This is the critical lesson we talked about in the last two sections.

But how can you relax and go into a low energy state?

Generally speaking, you are going to look for tension in your body, then release it. When that flash of fear strikes, you must learn to stop for a few seconds to be aware of how you're standing, what muscles you are tensing, what you're doing with your hands and/or feet, and what your facial expression is. A good strategy for achieving physical relaxation is to quickly start at the top of your head, consciously relaxing every muscle you can feel and control, then working your way down until you hit your toes.

Are the muscles in your forehead and around your eyes tense? Relax them.

Are you grimacing or clenching your jaw? Relax those muscles.

Are you craning your neck or straining it in any way?

Are your shoulders bunched up around your ears or hunched inward as if protecting against physical assault? Relax those areas.

Let the tension out of those muscles.

Are you clenching your fists ? Let go. Loosen your hands.

What are you doing with your arms? Relax them and put them down. There is no need to flail about, hug yourself, or hang on to any part of your body.

Let's move on to your torso and chest. This is a difficult area. You do not have direct control over the muscles in your chest wall. Even when you've let the tension out of the rest of your muscles, you may still feel as if there is a tight band around your chest. This is to be expected. You've felt it many, many times before and it has never hurt you, so you'll need to let that feeling be there and work on relaxing the muscles you can relax.

You do have control over the muscles in your back. These are the muscles responsible for your posture. Be aware of how you're standing or sitting and do your best to put yourself in a chest out, chin up position if possible. This is not critical, but "chest out, chin up" is a strength posture. Standing confidently feels differently than being rolled up into a ball.

Remain relaxed as you work on achieving a more confident yet non-resistive posture. Take a look at your abdominal muscles. Are they flexed and rock hard as if you're about to take a punch to the midsection? Let that go. Relax them completely. This is of special note because we are going to need these relaxed abs when we get to proper breathing.

What about the muscles in your lower body? You will be surprised at how quickly you will tense and contract your glutes—the muscles in your rear end. Are you doing that? Stop. Relax those muscles.

While you're down there, get your legs into a relaxed and neutral position. There's no need to grip your seat with your thighs or stand like you're about to run an Olympic sprint time trial. Let go of the tension in your quads, hamstrings, and calves. Let your legs fall naturally into position. It doesn't matter if you are seated, standing, or laying down. Let go and let them be in an unforced position.

Last, notice your feet and toes. Surprisingly, I have heard many people say that their feet are sore when anxious because they are standing and gripping the ground with their toes. If was a guessing kinda guy, I'd think that maybe this is some kind of ancient survival instinct, but that would be just a guess. Relax your feet and toes. You do not have to dig in like you're about to be blown over by a tornado.

One of the best descriptions I've ever heard of the state you're looking to achieve with your body is "rag doll." Scan for tension, release it, and shoot for "rag doll." It may take you time to achieve this in real-world conditions, but with enough practice you will get there.

Let's talk about practicing relaxing muscles while we're at it.

I suggest you learn about progressive muscle relaxation and practice it as often as you can. This is an easy exercise that involves intentionally flexing/tensing your muscles, feeling the tension, then releasing it. It's progressive because you start at one end of your body and end up at the other. Learning this exercise and repeating it as often as you can (it only takes a few minutes) will help you recognize what tension feels like and how to release it. When you practice, you get familiar with the state you are trying to achieve while getting better at the physical act of releasing your muscular tension. Practice this when calm so that releasing tension becomes mindless and automatic when in a panic state. This is important. You can't expect to only do these things when anxious or experiencing panic. You must practice them all the time to get good at them. Trust me, it's well worth the time.

I have some information and links to progressive muscle relaxation on my website, located here: https://theanxioustruth.com/skills.

Go there and see if what I am sharing helps you. It can't hurt!

The other aspect of physical relaxation and low energy state is speed. More specifically, not rushing. When anxious, most people tend to speed up, especially if you are trying desperately to escape back to your "safe zone." Speed is the enemy here. When anxious, not only do you have to learn to relax your body, but you also must be aware of rushing, and you must learn to move your body slowly and deliberately through space and time.

Rushing around makes things more frenetic and puts you into that higher energy state that we want to skip. Being a speed demon is an escape behavior and we know that we need to drop those behaviors, so slow down. Take each step slowly. Tie your shoes slowly and deliberately. Slow your words down. Slow your breathing down. You will do well to slow pretty much everything down when you feel panic rising. This is tricky mainly because you may not even realize that you are in high gear. Start to pay attention to that and do everything more slowly than you initially want to. There are no magic tricks here. Slowing down simply means...slowing down. You don't have to move at a snail's pace, just do not allow yourself to get into high-speed mode.

Breathing Properly

OK, so now we have your body in a more relaxed, lower-energy state. The next thing we want to look at is the breath. How many times have you been told, "just breathe," or "take a deep breath"? Probably thousands. It appears that the breath is the default when it comes to getting someone to "calm down." That's all well and good, but it's not that simple. It's not all that complicated either, but first you have to understand that the breath is not an instant panic killer. And a deep breath does not have anything to do with ratcheting down your level of anxiety.

Let me explain.

Taking a deep breath is good advice when you're angry at your spouse for leaving the cap off the toothpaste, but it's not good advice when you're dealing with panic attacks. It leads to anxious people desperately trying to fill their lungs to the brim with air, then blasting it all out in a heavy sigh. The tension in the chest muscles makes this feel impossible, yet they will try repeatedly. Giant breath, inflating the chest to an extreme degree, a short pause, then a rapid exhale of that entire volume of air. Repeated often enough, this can and often does lead to over-breathing, otherwise known as hyperventilation—resulting in too little carbon dioxide in the bloodstream. Hyperventilation causes tingling or numbness in the face, hands, and feet. In extreme cases, the hands and feet will cramp and lock into "claw-like" positions. If continued, hyperventilation can lead to fainting. While none of this is dangerous and is rapidly remedied by the body when allowed to breathe on its own again, these things are nonetheless frightening and disturbing—two complications that someone in the grips of panic absolutely does not need.

How should you be breathing?

When anxiety arrives and you feel panic building, relax your body like we talked about above. Make sure your shoulders are down and your abdominals are relaxed. Now breathe into your stomach. Do not move your chest or your shoulders. When you inhale, your stomach should rise and stick out from your body. When you breathe into your belly, you are expanding your diaphragm, making room for your lungs to expand. This is how your body is designed to breathe. Your ribcage is rigid, so trying to inflate your chest to get a "deep breath" is an exercise in futility. Relax your shoulders and chest, relax your stomach muscles, and breathe into your belly. It will feel much easier.

There is no need to take a giant breath. You do not have to totally fill your lungs with air. Your body doesn't need that. Just inhale into your belly gently, maybe counting slowly to 4 or 5. When you're done with the inhale, pause for a second, then SLOWLY exhale, counting to 5 or 6. Your exhale should be slightly longer than your inhale, so keep it slow. The object here is to avoid that heavy sigh. When you exhale slowly, you are controlling the level of carbon dioxide in your bloodstream and keeping it where it's supposed to be. This will help keep the feelings of unreality and confusion from getting away from you and will keep you from hyperventilating.

If you've been dealing with a numb face and numb fingers and toes when you get anxious, breathing properly is going to fix that for you almost immediately. I hear it from people all the time.

Repeat this pattern.

Inhale into your belly.

Pause.

Exhale slowly, longer than the inhale.

In through the nose.

Out through the nose if that's comfortable, but you can also exhale through your mouth so long as you keep your lips pursed to control the flow of air.

There really is no wrong way to do this, so whichever way is comfortable for you and keeps you in this gentle breathing pattern is fine.

In through the nose into the belly, pause, out through the nose slowly and longer than the inhale. It's a simple formula.

I have information and links to proper breathing tutorial videos on my website. You can find them at https://theanxioustruth.com/skills.

As with muscle tension release and relaxation, this breathing tactic should be practiced often. Learn the skill. Make it the automatic way you breathe all the time. Do not wait until panic strikes to decide that you want to breathe it away. Practice matters. It will make it easier for you to breathe properly when under pressure. This is why athletes practice before actual games and matches. If you can do it in practice, you can do it in a real competition. If you can properly breathe while sitting quietly at lunch, you can do it when in a total panic.

Learn it. Practice it. Use it.

I need to mention something else when it comes to the breath. When you search the internet to learn ways to breathe, especially if you are searching for terms like "breathing and anxiety," you are going to find some good resources that teach basic diaphragmatic breathing. You will also find resources that will veer way off into territory that I do not believe you need to be in. Spirituality aside for the moment—because we're trying to solve an actual practical problem here—please keep a few things in mind.

The breath is not magical. It holds no special power over anything in particular. Breathing is not the cure for anything, including your anxiety disorder. It's a bodily function that can contribute to both feeling worse, and feeling better, but it is not special or all-powerful. The breath is not linked to chakras or energy flows or the manifestation of anything in the universe. We do not care about these things at the moment. You may want to explore those concepts at some point. That's fine. For now, however, none of that is serving you in any way. Just stay focused on learning and mastering this simple breathing pattern for the pure mechanics of it. Trust me; that's all you need to go down the road to recovery.

Learning To Focus Productively

The last skill we need to talk about is the skill of focus.

Focusing is so important, yet so difficult to describe and teach well. So much of learning to fully experience anxiety and panic without fighting or fleeing is based on focus. When anxious, your mind will race. You may have obsessive and/or irrational thoughts. When in a panic, you will likely be gripped by irrational catastrophic thoughts that communicate to you that you are in danger and need to find escape and safety. Many people say that its thoughts, not physical sensations, that fuel their panic and anxiety. This is incredibly common. If we really boil it down, even physical sensations aren't a problem in and of themselves. The feeling of pain in the muscles of your chest isn't too bothersome unless it's accompanied by an interpretation of what's happening, aka your thoughts. So, in the end, what you are dealing with is all about thoughts. This is more obvious for some people than others, but it rings true regardless.

That being the case, the single most valuable skill you need to learn is how to place your focus where you want it to be at any given time. You already do this on a daily basis without realizing it. You choose to look at your phone rather than to actually listen to the person talking to you. You ignore the audiobook or podcast you have playing in the background because you want to check your Instagram, or because you're more interested in the dinner you're cooking. When your child is whining, you focus away from that because you don't want to reward him and teach the wrong lesson. You are already a focus machine. You just don't know it.

When anxiety rolls in, and panic rises, you forget your ability to direct your focus. You have thoughts, some of them really scary and uncomfortable, and you latch on to them. You debate them. You argue with them. You engage in internal conversations with them. They tell you to jump. You ask how high. You react to your anxious and fearful thoughts—irrational though they may be—as if you are required by some immutable law of nature to follow them wherever they may lead. This is simply not true. You are not required to follow nor honor every thought you have.

This is often a revelation to people.

They have often never considered the possibility that they don't have to follow those catastrophic, irrational, "oh my God" thoughts. When told that they can learn to focus elsewhere, they are usually elated...for a minute. Then they remember how loud and "powerful" those thoughts are. I'm often told, "I understand logically I'm not required to follow them, but I have no way to resist them." People can feel completely powerless over thoughts fueled by anxiety, panic, and fear. They can view these thoughts as monsters and invading armies. They are not armed to fight and not able to resist. When they come, it is a nightmarish disaster from which there is no escape.

This could not be more wrong. Your brain is an amazing computing machine and information processing powerhouse. It's unmatched to anything else we've discovered or invented up to now. Your brain is absolutely incredible. It has the power to reason and draw conclusions, then act upon those conclusions to bring about desired outcomes. In the case of this problem we are trying to solve, it works like this:

1. You understand and accept that anxious and fearful thoughts are just thoughts and that they do not represent reality. You come to grips with the fact that they are no more than irrational attempts to predict the future (be it five seconds or five days from now), and that they are ALWAYS wrong.

2. You conclude that to break free from the thoughts that fuel your anxiety and panic problems, you must learn to focus away from them and ignore them. You accept that you must no longer engage with them and follow them.

3. You work on the skill of placing your focus where you want it to be, even in the face of a tidal wave of anxious, fearful, irrational thoughts. You do this because you know that when you learn to pay them no mind, you will no longer be ruled by them.

The goal is not to make the thoughts go away. You will not be able to banish them with any kind of tricks or techniques. There is a massive amount of research in the behavioral sciences that shows pretty clearly that thought suppression does not work. You are not trying to change the thoughts into something different. Do not let anyone tell you that you should take those negative thoughts and somehow turn them into positive thoughts. That won't work. You cannot wrestle with or argue with irrational thoughts.

You are being reasonable, and by definition those thoughts are not. This is why you will never win those arguments.

You are not trying to soothe those thoughts with mantras or positive affirmations. They probably work well when you are calm, but when in the middle of high anxiety or panic, the irrational mind will always get in the last word. Attempting to talk yourself off the ledge by repeating "I'm OK" or "Its only anxiety" will not work. There is always one more "what if" thought to be had. Trying to convince yourself that you're OK while not actually feeling OK can often make things even worse. Does this sound like a familiar thought to you: *why isn't this working???!!!!* I hear it often.

You are not trying to distract yourself from your anxious thoughts or drown them out. That is avoidance, and it will come back to bite you down the road. I am not going to tell you how to turn up the radio or call a friend to escape from those thoughts. When you do that, you are giving your thoughts power that they should never have. If you treat them like you must run from them, they will stalk you forever.

What you are attempting to do is to let loose those thoughts. Let them pop into your head. When they do, simply turn your back on them. Place your focus somewhere else—where you want it to be. I always strongly suggest placing your focus on the tip of your nose and on your breath. It's an easy target that you always have available.

When the fearful, negative thought comes, gently turn your back on it by focusing on your breath. Do NOT answer it. Acknowledge it for a second, then turn away. When it comes again, repeat this refocusing exercise, as many times as you have to. If another one comes, do the same thing. This is VERY hard to do. Learning to focus intentionally on something while your brain is SCREAMING scary things in your face is not easy at all. I said earlier that hard is not the same as impossible. *You can learn to do this. You can practice this. You can master this skill just like you can master any other skill.*

Does this mean that you are doomed to live the rest of your life trying to ignore the scary thoughts in your head? It does not mean that. As you get better at accepting that the thoughts will come, and at simply allowing them to be there without engaging with them, you will find that your thoughts will become softer. They won't seem as loud or powerful any longer. When you master the skill of selective, intentional focus, you will find that what you once viewed as an irresistible force will seem insignificant in your life. In time, you'll even be able to intentionally examine those thoughts that once terrified you. You'll be able to deconstruct them and play with them like toys. They will no longer matter, and you will no longer be their hostage.

Once upon a time, I was unable to even see words like "dead," "death," or "die." I was so afraid and obsessed with the idea of death, dying, and non-existence, that I even forbid my then-young daughters to use those words. They would send me in a tailspin. Well, it was my reaction to those words that was doing that, but you get the idea. Now, after becoming an expert at not allowing irrational thoughts and fears to dictate to me, I am easily able to sit at any time and ponder my own existence, my own mortality, and lots of other pretty deep issues. This causes me no anxiety or stress. I am unafraid. I even quite enjoy discussing those concepts sometimes. Thoughts that were once my enemies are now my toys. This can happen for you too.

I'm often asked if it's better to sit, lie down, or just keep going with "life" when anxiety and panic strike. The answer isn't always clear. When it comes to the focus part—learning to focus away from your scary thoughts—you may have to start by sitting down or at least standing still. It might be easier for you to focus on your nose and breath that way in the beginning. That's perfectly acceptable.

As you improve your ability, you will find that you can focus on your nose and breath while in motion. As you get even better, you will find that you don't even need your nose or breath. You'll be able to use other items or even ongoing tasks as effective, purposeful focus points. This is a learning process. As with any learning process, things change and evolve over time. If need be, start by sitting or lying. When you get good at that, you can move forward and adjust what you need to do, or what you want to do. There's no rush here.

I STRONGLY suggest you learn basic meditation skills to assist with this. Did I say STRONGLY? I mean it.

The basics of meditation are all about focus—usually learning to focus on your breath and ignoring everything else. A beginner course in meditation will be all about letting thoughts come and go without judging them, engaging with them, or building a story around them. This is essentially a focus skill. Focus on the thoughts, or on your breath? You get to choose which one.

There are many, many excellent resources to help you learn basic meditation and focus skills. I've compiled a list, along with links to some great tutorials, apps, and classes on my website at https://theanxioustruth.com/skills. But like everything else we're talking about, you must make the effort to learn the skill, then practice it often. Every day. Multiple times every day. Just a few minutes at a time matters. Make the commitment to learn this skill and practice it. The benefits will be enormous both in your recovery and throughout the rest of your life. Being in control of your focus is a powerful thing that can be used beyond anxiety. Being a master of focus means you can switch from one task to another quickly and effectively. Strong focus allows you to home in on the true nature of problems rather than being distracted by ancillary issues. Well-developed focus skills make you more effective in times of crisis or emergency. I could go on about this.

Learning the skill of focus changes so much in life. I highly recommend it!

You may want to tell me now that you're just "not the meditating type." You may want to tell me that it doesn't work for you, or that you can't do it because you can't sit still. Maybe you don't want to learn basic meditation because you can't stand the thought of being silent with your thoughts. I understand these are all challenges, but many things worth doing are challenging.

We are trying to solve this anxiety problem, and learning these skills are a part of that.

Remember also that we are LEARNING these skills. You may be very bad at meditation and focus now, but that's OK. You will get better with practice...if you practice!

So, embrace it.

You can't break free from scary thoughts and at the same time declare that you just aren't cool with learning how.

If I ask you how to change the color of my walls from gray to blue, you will tell me to paint them. If I tell you that painting just isn't for me, then the conversation is over, and I will have to live with gray walls. If you want this to work, you have to drop your preconceived notions about meditation and what it is and isn't. It's not spiritual (for our purposes), nor is it about going deep inside to find yourself. It can be, but it's not by default and that's not how you'll get the best use out of it—or the way that you need to use it. Accept that meditation—as I am describing it—is really a focus exercise. What I'm asking you to do is learn how to focus. That doesn't seem too bad, does it?

Let's also touch on mindfulness while we're here.

Mindfulness—the practice of living in every moment rather than in the past or future—is also about focus. It has tremendous value for those of us trying to solve our anxiety problem. When you learn basic meditation and focus skills, which you learn while at rest, the next step is to put your meditation literally into motion.

Mindfulness as meditation in motion is nothing more than honing the ability to break things into the smallest possible steps, focusing fully on each step before moving on to the next. Mindfully brushing one's teeth is a place to start (understanding that you don't have to actually brush until you get to that part). There are probably 10 preliminary steps to brushing your teeth (gripping the toothbrush, picking it up, gripping the toothpaste, opening the cap, etc.) that come first before you get to the brushing. Each of them is as important and worthy of full focus as much as the actual brushing part.

Mindfulness almost forces you to slow things down, which is always a good thing as we've discussed.

As you get better at basic focus skills, i.e., basic meditation skills, you will go from dealing with anxiety and panic in a stationary position to being able to deal with it while on the move without even missing a beat. You will naturally learn to put your focus not necessarily on your nose and breath while you sit, but you can put it on whatever activity you are engaged in.

With enough practice, you will naturally use the principles of mindfulness to be non-reactive in the face of extreme anxiety and even panic. Sure, your thoughts will scream at you, but you will no longer care. After a while, they will no longer scream. And THAT will be a good day.

I promise.

Before we move on to the next lesson, I need to acknowledge that a full course in meditation and/or mindfulness is well beyond the scope of this book. I can give you the basics as I've done here, but actively engaging with other resources to learn and sharpen these skills is going to be important for you. So make sure you do a little credible research to improve this skill. Yes, you will need it.

Lesson 3.8

Persistence and Patience

The process of being aware of your reactions and changing them while going INTO the fear requires three things. They are important. Write them down. I mean, they're already written down here but write them down anyway. Stick them on your refrigerator or mirror if you need to.

Be tenacious.

Be persistent.

Be patient.

Tenacity. Get some. You have to really want this, to the point where you are entirely OK with the idea that you are going to do hard, scary things repeatedly and on purpose. Then get prepared for days when you feel like it's not working, for days when you don't want to do the work, and for days when you just want it all to go away once and for all.

This is normal and to be expected. You must not allow these less-than-perfect days to throw you off the path. Tenacity means being discouraged but not beaten. It means trusting the process and executing your plan even when you're unsure of how to get off the sofa. Tenacity means hearing people cast doubt upon what you're doing but ignoring what you hear and pressing forward. Tenacity involves sometimes going against conventional wisdom and instinct, hard though that may be to do.

Knowing when it's time to put on blinders and engage laser focus is part of being tenacious. Accepting that you will get back on your feet after your rest periods, then doing it, even though the idea of prolonged retreat seems so appealing—that's being tenacious. Embracing the idea that you must be afraid and uncomfortable now so that you can be unafraid and free later is being tenacious. Keeping your eyes on the goal and learning to not fear how you feel is being tenacious.

Being tenacious means taking what you think is a failure and turning it around. It means going back to the failure point and doing it again, even when all you want to do is hide. Being tenacious means that failure is not an option and that even in the darkest moments, you will remind yourself to see the hidden lessons and positives.

Tenacity isn't always easy. Giving up takes less effort. Retreating is more comfortable. Making excuses is simpler and offers immediate relief. Some people aren't wired to be naturally tenacious, but that doesn't mean it's impossible. Tenacity is sometimes about the sheer force of will, and everybody has that inside them. Use it when needed.

Be tenacious, even when you don't want to be or think you can't. Trust me; it will matter along your path to recovery. It will teach you lessons you will be grateful for many years down the road.

Be persistent.

You must do this work every day with no days off.

When I decided I was done living a small life based on fear, I dragged my rear end out of bed every single day and immediately got in my car to drive. I started in such a small way, but that counted. I did this religiously—even multiple times every day—for months. When things got comfortable, it was time to try something harder or new, so I did. I took no days off, gave myself no excuses, and feared no obstacles. I just did what I knew needed to be done day in and day out. It was that simple.

That is persistence.

One of the first rules of persistence is that you must prioritize your recovery above all else. That's not selfish or self-centered. It's utterly necessary. Being persistent means that you make time for yourself to work on your recovery plan and that the time is non-negotiable. The time may shift from one day to the next, but the time is always taken. You can't be persistent if you put the kids, your spouse, your job, your cat, or your Instagram account first. You can only be persistent in your recovery when you put *yourself* first. While this may go against your natural instincts and tendencies, you're going to have to do it anyway. Be persistent and non-negotiable with the time you need to do the work now so that you can be selfless and giving again later when you're back to "normal."

I would strongly suggest scheduling your exposures and the recovery work you need to do. Put it on your calendar. This helps formalize your plan and your commitment. It can go a long way toward not "taking it easy" on the days that you don't feel like doing the work. *Sorry dude, it's on your calendar, so it's time to lace up and get in the game!*

Persistence is one of the qualities missing in the vast majority of recovery plans, especially when starting out.

Persistence means that you do the work regardless of how you feel. If you're in bed with a high fever and can't stop coughing and sneezing, by all means, take the day off and get better. But if you're in bed because you're afraid, worried, or you're not comfortable with going out that day, GET UP. Do it anyway.

Making excuses and putting things off until tomorrow because you're having a less than great day isn't part of your plan anymore. Going into the fear only when you're having a "good day" isn't effective and is also no longer part of your plan. This process isn't random or spur of the moment. It's calculated and requires planning and commitment.

Hard code persistence into your recovery plan, and do not let yourself off the hook. You'll be proud of yourself for doing it and happy that you did.

Be patient. This is not a linear process.

You will not banish your anxiety and panic problems in a few days or even a few weeks. It takes time.

Sadly, we can learn a phobic behavior almost instantly, but we simply do not un-learn it at the same rate. This is a process of persistence and repetition. Some days will be excellent and full of noticeable progress. Some days will be slow and full of bad feelings and scary sensations. You'll feel like you're going backward. But you're never going backward. Patience, grasshopper. You need those days more than you need the good days. I promise.

So long as you don't retreat and don't fall into the trap of telling yourself a failure story, you're learning and moving forward even if the steps are tiny.

Here's a bit of good news if you are sure that I'm some kind of relentless, heartless anxiety recovery terminator cyborg. It's OK, I've heard it before. Patience is the part where you can be kind and compassionate to yourself. Understanding that this process takes time and that you will make mistakes, and being OK with those mistakes, is part of patience. Getting frustrated because you're not going faster doesn't help you. Part of learning patience is being OK with the fact that this is a journey. There are lessons to learn and experiences to have along the way, all of which will become part of you forever. They will go well beyond your anxiety issues.

When you want to call yourself a failure because you're still feeling panic, stop.

Remember that you're supposed to feel panic as part of this process. Don't berate yourself for getting it wrong. Think objectively about what's happening and learn to see the lessons in front of you. This isn't about being faster or slower, right or wrong, or better or worse. This is about trusting the process—trusting your plan and letting it unfold in whatever time it takes to unfold.

Appreciate what you're doing.

Be proud of the effort you're putting forth and the courage you're finding and displaying. Admire your own tenacity and persistence. Know that you're better today than you were yesterday or two months ago. Stop seeing yourself as a person crippled with panic, fear, and anxiety. The day you took step one in the right direction, you stopped being that person. You're different—better—every day after having taken that first step.

So, be patient. Not only because you have no other choice, but because you've earned the right to be.

In the end, tenacity, persistence, and patience are a potent combination. Ruthless drive and unflinching commitment with a side order of self-compassion is a tough combination to beat. So before we move on to the next chapter and start actually crafting a recovery plan, take time to conjure up some tenacity, persistence, and patience ...then let's go!

CHAPTER 4

MAKING YOUR

RECOVERY PLAN

Lesson 4.1

This is a DOING Thing

Now it's time to create your recovery plan.

But before you do, you need to understand one critical concept.

Solving this problem is a DOING thing that requires ACTION. This is not thinking, reading, talking, debating, or considering. Your recovery plan will be based on DOING things that you probably don't want to do. Remember, the doing is the secret sauce that makes it all happen. Without taking action—real observable behavioral action—none of what we're talking about matters.

Consider the idea of being thirsty. You want a glass of water. You can think about the water and the glass. You can talk about being thirsty. You can talk about drinking water. You can learn everything there is to learn about the molecular structures of water and glass. You can ponder the philosophy of half empty or half full glasses of water. You can debate the merits of different water filters, water delivery systems, and drinking vessels. You can stockpile an impressive array of inspirational quotes and memes involving water and thirst. You can imagine 19 different ways that one might approach the task of getting a glass of water. You can dream about water, wish you had water, and pray to a higher power to provide you with life-sustaining water. You may choose to write poems and stories about water and thirst. There are likely some internet forums you can join where there is endless discussion on the topic of drinking water.

You can do all these things from now until the sun burns out. But until you actually get up, fill that glass with water, and drink, you will still be thirsty.

The same applies to recovering from an anxiety disorder and solving this problem we're addressing. You're going to have to ACT. No amount of reading, thinking, pondering, debating, framing, re-framing, considering, discussing, or visualizing is going to get you out of the situation you are in. What will get you out of this situation is DOING. Let's look at why only acting and doing will get this job done.

The part of your brain responsible for the fear and panic response does not respond to logic, reason, or language. You may have heard the terms "lizard brain" or "primitive brain." Both terms imply something more simplistic is at work in your brain, which is accurate. Your brain's fear center is there to keep you alive and safe. It isn't concerned with language, logic, reasoning, ideas, morals, ethics, or spirituality. It doesn't even understand those concepts. The fear center in your brain can't be spoken to. It doesn't understand words, images, or diagrams. It doesn't listen to song lyrics or know what memes are. The concepts of inspiration and wishing and hoping do not exist in your fear center. To sum up, you cannot communicate with your fear center. It's simply not listening and doesn't care what you have to say.

Your fear center knows one thing...experience.

You can't TELL your lizard brain anything. You have to SHOW it. Taking action. Doing. Getting in the car even though that scares you. Going to the mall even though that scares you. Refusing to check your heart rate or blood pressure, even though that scares you.

Remember, our job is to teach your brain some new lessons. We need to show it that even when you are in a panic, you are safe. We are not on a mission to banish anxiety from your life. Our missing is to teach your brain—

the fear center specifically—that you no longer have to fear anxiety, panic, and everything that comes with it.

The catch is, if you plan to teach your brain this lesson, you must SHOW it. You must give it experiences to learn from. You will never successfully tell it. It's not getting the messages. You've likely been trying to talk, reason, and think your way out of this situation for a very long time without success, so this is not news to you. It is frustrating and annoying, and it means that all the books you've read, videos you've watched, and discussions you've participated in have not changed things for you in any meaningful way.

How do we show the fear center in our brain that it no longer has to be afraid of anxiety and panic? How do we teach it that it's been wrong all this time?

It's a simple sequence:

Enter a situation that makes you anxious or even panic. Do it in a planned way.

Let the sensations, thoughts, and fear come. Experience all the anxiety. Experience panic if that's what happens. This is critical. You MUST experience whatever comes at you.

DO NOT REACT. SURRENDER!

DO NOTHING!

You will go into anxious situations and experience all the unpleasant, scary, uncomfortable things that you hate, but you must remain committed to not reacting. Understand that you won't fight, brace, run, flee, or avoid. You will engage in none of your old safety rituals. You will lay yourself wholly bare and open to the onslaught that you fear so much. There will be no protection and no attempt to save or protect yourself.

Here's where the magic happens. You will be OK. No harm will come to you. It never has before, and it will not now. The key is that your brain will experience fear and discomfort AND a positive outcome. This will happen WITHOUT all the safety, avoidance, and escape tricks of the past. Your fear center will experience a positive outcome without actively creating that outcome. This happens by sitting and being afraid and uncomfortable. And even though you will feel this way, you will still wind up OK, despite the fact you've done absolutely nothing in response to the fear. This is how you teach your brain a new lesson.

After enough repetition, practice, and repeated positive outcomes, your brain is going to stop sounding the alarm. It will start to sound much more reasonable. Imagine the day that your brain says, "Hey, that was no fun, but it wasn't actually dangerous. I may have been wrong about this whole thing." That day will come.

When you go into the fear, experience it fully without trying to save yourself, learn you will be OK, and repeat that experience often in a planned, repetitive, incremental systematic way. When you do this, you are teaching your brain the new lessons it needs to replace the old lessons. You are showing it that it's been wrong all this time. You are providing your lizard brain with the experiences it requires to change its tune regarding anxiety, panic, and all the associated feelings and thoughts that come with it.

We are identifying the same cognitive mechanism that got you into trouble, putting it in reverse, then using it to get you out of trouble. It's a fantastic concept, but as you can see, this requires actual experience. This requires action. Doing. Not talking. Not thinking. Just doing. Without action, it does not work.

At this point, I would like to address an issue I see raised all the time. The issue of "being ready" or finding something that "clicks" with you before you take action. I have seen thousands of people stay on the sidelines, out of the recovery game, because they refuse to act.

They do all the thinking, talking, discussing, and everything else, but they do not act. Often they will tell me that I am telling them to do something terrifying (this is true) and that before they can bring themselves to do it, they have to find a way to convince themselves that it's not scary. They search for some way to frame the idea or conceptualize it so that it "clicks" with them. I am literally asked, "How am I supposed to do this when I do not believe that I am safe?" Here's the straight answer. You will NEVER be ready to do this.

You will never believe that you are safe until you show your fear center that you are. No mental or emotional shift happens to make you ready to go do hard, scary things. There may be a shift at a motivational level, but on a fear level, you are never going to wipe away the fear before acting. You act first, even though you are terrified, then you learn that you are safe.

It's the action—the doing—that teaches you the fear has been baseless all this time.

I am often both frustrated and saddened to see people spend so much time and effort trying to "get OK" with what they have to do when what they're really trying to do is eliminate the fear before they act. This is backward, and it's a colossal waste of time and effort to go down this road. You don't need one more book, video, or program to find the magic formula. You need action.

Remember—above all else—that fear and danger are not the same things.

We are talking about doing things that will make you afraid and uncomfortable, but that are in no way dangerous or unsafe. I am NEVER asking you to do unsafe things. Your brain just hears it that way.

Even if you are ready to act from a motivational standpoint, if you are prepared to do what it takes to get your life back and solve this problem, you will still be very afraid to do what you need to do as part of your recovery plan. That is normal and to be expected. Being motivated isn't the same as being unafraid. You might feel highly motivated while also being highly afraid. You must act anyway—despite the fear—to lose the fear. That's the definition of being brave—acting even when scared—that's how this process works.

As I've done so many times, I am going to ask you to take a little time again to consider what you've just read. Are you totally on board with the idea that you will only solve this problem by doing? Are you OK with the fact that you will be doing hard and scary things that will make you uncomfortable? Are you willing to be brave—especially in the beginning? Are you going to be able to act even when you are afraid to act? You have to get yourself into this mindset before moving forward for this to be most effective.

I understand what I am sharing with you may sound crazy. If you need to go back and read this section a few times again or review the theory from the last chapters, I understand.

This is not a race. Take the time you need to be clear on what you need to do so that you can move forward with confidence in your direction.

Oh, and because I know you will likely ask, I am not telling you that you must endure fear and discomfort intentionally for the rest of your life. You don't have to live the life of some kind of superhero. You will learn to not fear anxiety and panic, and then everything will change. The rest of your life is not going to be a blindfolded rollercoaster ride from hell, so please don't imagine it that way.

Lesson 4.2

This Takes Time

One more short lesson before we get down to the business of how to create a recovery plan.

This takes time. Please understand and accept this. You're going to have to be patient. You are simply not going to go from being agoraphobic (for example) to living the "normal" life you've imagined for yourself in seven days. That's just not the way this works. I know that might sound disappointing, but it is reality. I am not going to promise you miracles that don't exist.

Sadly, human beings can develop a phobia or intense fear almost instantly. You've experienced this firsthand. Also, unfortunately, we can't unlearn those phobias as quickly. Especially in the case of your particular problem, an anxiety disorder, the need for systematically and incrementally repeating experiences with positive outcomes means that this process will take some time. If you've been primarily homebound for the last four months and will only go out with a safe person, it's quite possible for you to learn to drive your kids to school or shop at a local shop for a few items within a couple of weeks. That can absolutely happen. I've seen it.

While that's far better than being stuck at home, that is not being recovered. Your initial progress, even when rapid, will feel tenuous, fragile, and unsure at times. You may marvel at how you've gotten yourself into the school pick-up routine, but you will probably still be nervous and shaky while doing it, and you will likely still view a trip to the shopping mall as near impossible. This is normal. Expect it.

One of the most common reasons I see for "failed" recovery is an unrealistic timeline. You may get highly motivated and ready to take your life back. Excellent, but don't let this lead to unrealistic expectations. I've seen many people get two weeks into the process, complain that they're still feeling anxiety, and then declare it useless. I've also seen people experience a near anxiety-free day, assume everything is fixed, then crash hard when it comes back a day or two later. Don't do this to yourself.

My own recovery was every bit a 6-8-month process to get me probably 80 percent of the way toward living a "normal" life. The remaining 20 percent took much longer because it involved doing things that were simply not a regular part of daily life (long trips, flying, etc.). I was an unstoppable, undeniable exposure and recovery machine that never took a day off, and it still took me months to attain solid footing in situations that I found fearful. You are not going to accept this plan, do a few things, and be fixed in two weeks.

I get asked all the time, "How long will it take?"

The answer is, "However long it takes."

That's not being facetious. That's being realistic. Giving yourself a specific deadline is a bad idea. This is especially true if that deadline is based on some planned event or life change. Life is going to happen, but just because you have a wedding to fly to 3000 miles away in three months doesn't mean you are going to be recovered in three months.

The fear center in your brain doesn't have a calendar. It doesn't care about what you have coming up. It will work on its own time in its own way. Start with being OK with having at least a few months of hard work in front of you, then let it flow from there for however long it takes.

Try to keep in mind that you're not just solving your anxiety problem here. You are learning skills and lessons that will change your life in other ways, too. That makes every single day worth it. If it means that you need 200 days instead of 100 days, then that's worth it also. You are building more than just an anxiety solution every day. You are making a new and improved version of you. Is that something you think should happen in two weeks?

Let's talk about a common issue relating to timeline. The problem of the "setback" or "relapse." Get the idea of having a setback out of your head right now.

Your progress will not be linear. You will make great strides at times. Other times you will struggle. You will find that a task you declared conquered three weeks ago is making you anxious again. You may find that even months down the road, fundamental issues will resurface. You may be tempted to declare yourself "back to square one."

When you declare a setback or going backward, it means that you have lost sight of the goal you are working on. You have forgotten that this process takes time.

Remember, you are not working toward never feeling anxiety ever again. You are working toward being able to experience anxiety and panic without going into a five-alarm response mode to save yourself.

That takes time.

So when you're five months in or nine months in, and you wake up feeling anxious for the first time in weeks or months, please remember that this is both normal and OK. You're still working on it. Feeling anxious or experiencing panic again means you get to practice your skills again. This is a good thing when you remember the real goal and the long-term nature of this process.

Over time, and with repetition, you will become extremely well aligned with the real goal. You will become confident in your ability to react properly when anxiety makes a return visit. I know I keep asking you to trust me, but I'm going to ask you again to do that.

Trust me. Do what I am telling you. This is ALL going to get better.

I told you this would be short. About 1000 words. I didn't lie.

Get your patience in order. Get your expectations of a timeline in order, and then you are ready to make an actual recovery plan!

Lesson 4.3

Let's Set Some Goals

Without goals, there is no plan. It is not enough to say you want to get better in vague terms. You must be clear about what you want to accomplish along the road to recovery.

What would you like to be able to do again?

What do you really miss?

Which current anxiety-driven limitations are having the most significant impact on your life day-to-day?

Which fear-based patterns and behaviors would you like to break and remove from your life?

When you've reached that magical "normal" state again, what have you always dreamed of doing or accomplishing?

These are your goals. They are the specific tasks, actions, places, and situations that you will systematically and incrementally work toward as you execute your recovery plan.

Your goals must be well defined, well understood, and measurable. When setting your recovery goals, leaving too much room for subjective interpretation is a mistake. It leads to incorrectly declaring a failure. It can create needless negative self-judgment. It can result in over-estimating achievement and can also be an impediment to long-term progress.

It is not enough to say, "I want to drive again." That is vague and leaves your progress open to interpretation and emotional judgment. The better goal is, "I want to drive by myself to the beach." This is clear, easy to understand, and is not open to interpretation. Did you get to the beach? You did it! Didn't make it to the beach? Keep working.

When you phrase your goals in this way, there's no danger of misjudging success or failure. It minimizes the chance of harshly judging yourself for no reason. When solving this problem of ours, objectivity is essential! We need to take the emotion out of the process to as high of a degree possible.

Now let's look at setting immediate goals, mid-range goals, and long-term goals. This is useful in prioritizing things and keeping your recovery plan organized and easier to execute. If you're having a hard time walking around your neighborhood, setting a world cruise as your first goal isn't terribly useful. You'll work on your near-term goals first, and progress from there.

Immediate near-term goals will have the most impact on your daily life. They are the tasks and activities that you've been avoiding every day. They have had the most significant impact on your daily routine, your family, and the people around you.

Examples of immediate goals are being home alone for a few hours, driving the kids to school and back, and doing the grocery shopping. These are commonly avoided tasks that can have a significant impact on personal and family life over time. Additional immediate goals might include going out to dinner or a movie with your partner or family or attending a relative's birthday party. When selecting immediate goals, try to find what you can work on that will result in significant change in your life. This change comes by building a sense of basic competency and control. Lowering your stress level, and that of your friends and family members can also bring about significant change.

If you've been relying on family members and friends to handle the basics of life for you, doing these tasks yourself builds confidence and makes life less stressful for your loved ones. When you do this, they might be more likely to get behind you and your recovery plan.

Resist the temptation to let the family or social calendar dictate your immediate goals. If you've been living in a limited "safe zone" for any period, your only job is to break out of that safe zone in small increments. The fact that you have a wedding to attend in two months should not enter into this right now. Your immediate goal is not to get to that wedding. Your immediate goal (for example) is to be able to walk out the door or get coffee with your best friend without being terrified and gritting your teeth the whole time. Accomplish that, and you'll be surprised at how the wedding gets a bit easier to deal with, too!

Your recovery plan should also include eliminating the rituals and behaviors you've been automatically engaging in as a response to how you feel. When creating your list of immediate goals, you should also be identifying and extinguishing these rituals and behaviors. Examples might include continually holding your head in your hands, shielding your eyes from the light, retreating to be alone, or obsessively using your phone to distract you from how you're feeling.

Mid-range goals are things you want to be able to do again, but that don't happen regularly (i.e., vacations, family reunions, weddings, etc.). They require more of a leap out of your current "comfort zone" (i.e., returning to full-time work or school). As it pertains to going back to work or school, you may feel like you need to accomplish it soon as possible. I understand this, but it always makes the most sense to build small things first.

Then build larger things on top of those small things. You're starting your recovery from a place where you've been unsure, afraid, confused, and likely not very confident in yourself. Let's use small goals like the school pick-up run or going for a walk in the park to get you back onto firmer ground. Then you can jump back into the deeper waters of trips, work, school, and that sort of thing.

I realize this may not be an option for you. Life has to happen while you recover. Events come up and decisions must be made. My advice is to focus on immediate goals as much as possible. While working on your daily goals, if something in the mid-range does come up that you can't avoid, just do your best to handle it without fearing how you will feel and judging your success or failure based on how you felt while doing it. If possible, move those things back a while to give yourself the best chance of having the best experience and outcome when you do venture into that middle range of recovery.

Long term goals are huge items and events.

They might seem utterly impossible today.

Don't worry, they will be possible. Your long terms goals could be categorized as highly impactful life-changing event. This list might include a career path change, quitting work to return to school, starting a family, or moving far from where you currently live.

When identifying long term goals, remember that many of them can likely cause stress, worry, and even anxiety for any human being. Do not judge yourself harshly if making your long-term goals list upsets you. You may be tempted to declare them impossible and to tell yourself that you will never be able to even attempt them. These are just thoughts. Thoughts do not have to be honored, followed, or validated all the time. Write your long-term goals list in "brain dump" fashion. Don't overthink the details of the items you are including. Get it all out on the paper (or digital paper, as the case may be these days). Don't get caught up in ruminating on it. Then simply, file it away. You can do this because long-term goals are—well, for the long term. We don't have to concern ourselves with them too much right now.

Many people make the mistake of thinking that they can keep track of recovery goals in their heads. Try not to do this, as it leaves too much room for emotionally charged, subjective appraisal of progress (we want to avoid this), and too much wiggle room that you will invariably use to get out of doing hard or scary things when you don't feel like doing them. Write things down. Hold yourself accountable and use your written plan as a reference whenever needed.

I've created a free downloadable worksheet that you can use to create your recovery goals list. The worksheet is in PDF format. Print it or fill it out on your computer. It's designed to help you list your recovery goals, and categorize them into immediate goals, mid-range goals, and long-term goals. The worksheet also provides spaces for you to prioritize your goals so you can start working on them in order.

Having this outline in writing somewhere will be extremely helpful to keep you on track, and to facilitate re-grouping and tweaking your plan from time to time.

Download the free recovery goals worksheet at https://theanxioustruth.com/downloads

Once you have your goals down, It's time to acknowledge that things change, and nothing is set in stone.

Circumstances change.

Things come up that we don't plan for.

We can't see into the future, which means that we have to be OK with being flexible when the need arises.

Goals can be adjusted when the circumstances warrant it. Periodically sitting down to evaluate progress and modify your goals list is encouraged. You may even find that something on your immediate goals list turns out to be much easier for you than expected and can be removed from the list.

You may find that something from the mid-range list needs to be moved up into an immediate position. As you start executing your plan, you may discover new goals at all levels that you hadn't thought of. Add them to the proper category in the list.

Change is expected. This is OK and even encouraged in many cases.

Do not view changes and adjustments as indications of failure, a setback or "doing it wrong." Plotting out this part of your recovery can be a fluid process. Accept it now, and you will make it easier on yourself as you move along.

Now, for some good news.

The goals you are setting and working toward are not totally isolated from each other. Every goal will have some carryover into your other goals. Those first few are going to be most difficult because you are starting from scratch.

When you get good at walking around the block (for example), it makes it easier to walk to the park. Walking to the park makes it easier to go to the supermarket or pick up the kids from school. This is an additive process. You are building. Every experience adds another brick. Waiting in line at the McDonald's drive-through might seem like a nightmare to you now. But as strange as it may sound, those walks up and down your street are making it easier to do the drive-through.

Each time you face fear and pass through it without resistance—regardless of the situation—you are making progress that will matter in all situations. Remember that the McDonald's drive-through isn't the problem. It's how you feel at the drive-through that matters. It's the same way you feel when leaving the house or trying to get through a meal at a restaurant.

All your many fears are really one fear: you are afraid of anxiety and panic and all their symptoms.

Face that fear in one situation, and you will get better at facing it in every case.

This is probably a good time to mention the topic of monophobia—the fear of being physically alone. If you are dealing with panic disorder and/or agoraphobia, there is a good chance that you have developed monophobia. If this is true, you will do anything you can to avoid being home alone.

This is very common. I was severely monophobic.

When you still see panic and anxiety as dangerous things you must avoid and be saved from, you not only avoid places and tasks that might trigger them, but you will also often refuse to be left alone.

Monophobia is not a special fear that requires unique treatment or attention. You are afraid to be alone because you fear your own body and thoughts. When alone, you fear that nobody will be there to "save" you when you need it. Monophobia is driven by the exact same fear that drives your panic disorder or agoraphobia. As you get better at going to the mall (for example), it will become easier to be left alone at the same time.

You may choose to address monophobia directly by intentionally being alone systematically and incrementally. This is perfectly acceptable and effective and will also have a positive impact on the rest of your goals list. You don't have to do that though. Many people find that monophobia resolves on its own as they advance in their overall recovery. This is because regardless of how you choose to trigger it — being alone or driving to the supermarket (for example), you are addressing the same fear all the time. Attack your monophobia directly or attack all the other issues. Either way, you'll find that being alone gets easier and easier for you. That was certainly my experience.

While we're discussing the big picture and the setting of goals, I need to address a bit of potentially bad news. Don't worry, It's not a disaster, but it should be mentioned and now is as good a time as any.

Many people find that once they start working on their first few goals, they begin to feel worse than they did before. This is very common, and there's a simple explanation.

When you start intentionally going into the fear you've been avoiding for so long, you are no longer hiding. All that avoidance, running, and returning to the safe zone has been a shield against the sensations you hate so much. When you stop avoiding and start facing, that shield drops. You will no longer carry "protection" around with you. The illusion of safety will be shattered, and you may find that you feel worse before you feel better.

It's essential to realize that you are not feeling WORSE. You are only feeling MORE.

Without a shield and the illusion of safety (remember that you never needed to be saved anyway), you suddenly have no place to hide from your anxiety and panic. Your safe places may no longer seem safe. Anxiety may follow you into places that it hasn't previously. Again, this does not make it worse. You are merely allowing anxiety to be in your face more of the time. This is temporary. It is a necessary part of recovery.

Thinking that you were safe at home, in your car, or with your partner, has been an error. That error must be uncovered and corrected. You must learn that you are safe everywhere all by yourself. This means first feeling unsafe in these places. When you follow the plan and allow this to happen without resistance, you will still be OK, and you will be providing your brain with the experiences and signals it needs to understand that being afraid and being unsafe are not the same thing.

Feeling more poses a problem for many people because they view it as a setback. They assume it means they are worse off than everyone else or that they're doing recovery wrong. That's not the case. This is merely what happens when you strip away the imaginary and false protection you've been lugging around for so long.

You must first be afraid to learn how not to be afraid.

Now that we have our initial goals set, we're ready to look at the nuts and bolts of breaking them into small steps. We need to do this to achieve what you once thought unachievable. In the next lesson, we'll focus on how to carve each goal into small chunks, then tackle them in an organized way for a maximum chance at a positive outcome.

Lesson 4.4

Breaking Things Into Small Pieces

Before we get into the mechanics of breaking your goals into small chunks, let's address an issue that often gets confused and twisted a bit.

The road out of your anxiety and panic problem is best traveled in small steps. This problem is not about "breaking free" by making giant leaps when you're feeling especially motivated. That would be great, but it very rarely works that way.

I encounter people daily who get fed up, resolve to make a change, then decide to immediately leap from homebound to that 8-hour wedding they didn't think they were going to be able to attend. Sometimes the experience is good— which is always lovely. But then it leads to disappointment when they discover that they are back to "square one" four days later after thinking they had cured themselves in one swipe.

Most times, the experience is terrible and winds up having the opposite effect—driving the anxiety sufferer deeper into retreat. This person gets even more discouraged because they "couldn't do it." They often wind up declaring that it was worse than they could have imagined. They may decide that they are better off just staying in hiding.

I realize you are impatient. You have been suffering for some time and missing out on life. You want it all to be over so you can be back to normal. I get that. I felt that way too. But you MUST be patient and work within the parameters of the human brain. Remember, we are throwing your misdirected learning gears into reverse to get you out of the hole you're in.

That means we have to work the process and we don't get to dictate the pace.

The ability of our brains to retrain using repetitive experiences with positive outcomes dictates the pace. You can impact the pace with motivation, consistency, and a decision to do the work every day as required. Still, you cannot demand that yourself or your brain get better" at any particular rate. It will happen as it happens.

One more word on this. Breaking your goals into small chunks and attacking them in sequence also keeps you from being overwhelmed by your own recovery plan. If you've made a list of short term, midrange, and long-term goals, there is a chance that you've looked at that list and felt like accomplishing everything was impossible. Maybe you've felt overwhelmed because it seemed like too many things to do. You may be overwhelmed because you're not exactly sure where to even start.

No worries.

You don't have to accomplish every goal at the same time. Start with the smallest item and make it even smaller. Tiny steps taken repetitively, incrementally, and consistently will add up to all those items on your goals list. I promise it will.

OK, Let's get down to the business of the lesson.

You've got your goals listed, so let's start with your immediate goals. These are the tasks and situations you've been avoiding that have had the most impact on your life. Fixing these things will improve your overall experience in a significant way, so let's work on them first.

Pick one item from your list. This should probably be the smallest item. For our purposes, let's use a walk around your block as an example of a goal. We will build up to a walk around the neighborhood that right now may seem almost impossible.

A walk around the block may be an actual goal for you, or it may seem like a silly goal if you're able to do more than that. The walk isn't the point. I am merely using it to illustrate how to break a goal into small chunks. Follow along and apply the logic to whatever the first item on your goals list might be.

We'll use the concept of "fear ladders" to break how you're going to accomplish your goals. A fear ladder is a concept used by behavioral therapists to help you build to a conclusion by taking small, less fear-inducing steps toward that conclusion. Those steps are taken repetitively and sequentially in such a way that when you add them together, you'll have "climbed a ladder" to reach your goal. Each rung of the ladder is represented by the smaller steps you've taken toward that goal. A fear ladder is often used to prioritize your list of goals, but we can use the concept to break down each individual goal, too. It's a ladder of ladders!

If you want to take a walk around your block, Let's break that into a fear ladder as follows.

1. Plan your walk. Commit to exactly when you are going to take your walk and put it on your calendar. Consider for a few seconds that you will go out the door and walk around the block regardless of how you feel. Does this make you anxious? Does the mere act of thinking about this commitment make your heart race? Are you already feeling that familiar fear? This is good. It means you've correctly picked this task as the first rung on your fear ladder for this goal. Sit with those feelings. Let your heart race. Let the fear be there. Let your body and mind do whatever they want to do in response to your new commitment to take a walk, but do not react when it happens. Use your tools. Relax your body. Breathe. Place your focus where you want it—not inward on the sensations and thoughts. Just be there. The feelings might last a while. Let them. It's OK. This is your first step toward recovery! When the sensations begin to subside, stay in your relaxed state as best you can, and go about the rest of your business. Do not think about or focus on your upcoming walk. You can focus on it when you want

to focus on it, not when the irrational fear tells you to. Refocus away from it every time you find yourself thinking about it in a fearful way. You may have to do this many, many, many times. It may be tiring. This is OK. It's to be expected. In an hour or two, go back to your calendar and allow yourself to think about your upcoming walk again. Feeling anxious? I'm not surprised. Again, let it happen. Let it all come without reacting. You can't control the feelings and thoughts, but you can control your reaction to them. Stay cool, relax, breathe, and focus. When things start to calm down again, leave your calendar, and focus elsewhere on life again for a couple of or hours, then repeat the process. Can you see what we're doing? We're not walking yet. We're not even out the door yet. We're working on acclimating to the feelings you get just from thinking about taking that walk. You will have to assess how long this will have to last. If you can plan your walk and commit it to your schedule without feeling much discomfort, then you can move along to the next step on the fear ladder right away. If you're in a total panic at the mere idea of walking around the block, then you'll have to stay here and repeat this process in a systematic way for however long it takes to acclimate to it. This might be hours. It might be days. It doesn't matter. From a practical standpoint, if you think it might take you four days to get past this step, then plan your walk for four days from now. Remember when I said you need to be open to adjustment? This is what I mean. If you find that by day two you're feeling calm when you sit down to think about the walk, then go ahead and move it up on the calendar and to the next rung on the ladder.

2. It's time to get ready to take your walk. This means getting out of bed, off the sofa, or wherever you are stationary. Then getting dressed appropriately, putting on your shoes, and going to the door. This is the next rung on the fear ladder you will climb to accomplish your goal of walking around your block. Your plan is to execute the steps required to get from stationary to standing at the door, and to execute them SLOWLY and mindfully while keeping your

body relaxed, breathing properly, and maintaining your focus squarely on the task at hand. This may be combing your hair or putting on or tying your shoes. It may be brushing your teeth. Whatever those specific steps/tasks are that must be done to get to the front door and ready to walk out, do them in a relaxed, deliberate, focused, and mindful way. Are you getting anxious as you do it? Good. You need that to happen to retrain your brain. Let the sensations and thoughts come but do not react to them or follow them. Use your tools. It is expected and OK for you to feel very anxious and to even to panic as you get ready to take your walk. Failure isn't defined by the presence of anxiety. Just go through the steps and get yourself to the door. Was that pretty easy? Then move to the next rung on the ladder. If you found it very difficult to get to your door, then your work is done for now. Unwind your steps, relax, breathe, and regroup. You've done your job. There's no more need to focus on the walk or the getting ready part. Go back to your regularly scheduled life. You've accomplished what you need to accomplish. After a couple of hours (if practical), go through this exercise again. Prepare for your walk as if you are going to leave the house and do it. Run this drill as many times as is practical throughout the day. Repeat for as many days as you need to acclimate to this behavior. Repetition and consistency are your friends here. Do not worry about how many times you have to repeat or how many days it takes. Reschedule your walk 100 times if you have to. Learning to do this task without going off the rails is part of your recovery. You may have a hard time believing it, but this little exercise will actually help you get on an aircraft and fly around the world one day (if that is something you aspire to do). As with step one, when you're ready, It's time to go up the ladder!

3. Walk out your door. Now that you are comfortable thinking about the walk and getting ready to take your walk, It's time to take the next step—actually leaving the house and going outside. You're dressed and ready, so open the door and step outside.

Remember, this is the next step up on the fear ladder, so you are going to feel anxiety. You may even panic. Do not despair. You worked hard to get to that door. You are NOT a failure because stepping through the door is causing you to feel anxious or afraid. Again, this is supposed to happen. This is how you learn that It's OK to be afraid and uncomfortable. Remember when you couldn't even think about taking that walk? Now here you are standing outside! This is where you have to assess how you are. If you are in near panic just standing on the other side of the door, then plan to stay there in your usual relaxed, breathing, focused, non-reactive state for 60 seconds. Then go back in. Unwind. Relax. Regroup. By now, you know the drill. You will repeat this little exercise as many times as you can each day, for as many days as you need, to acclimate to walking out the door. If you can walk out the door without too much trouble, then good for you! Move on to the next step. If not, that's perfectly OK. Just repeat, repeat, repeat—using your tools to not react to the sensations and thoughts—until this gets easier for you, then move on. As always, it doesn't matter how many times or how many days it takes. Keep rescheduling that walk as required. As long as you are doing this work and moving toward your goal, everything is good.

4. Next step: start walking! This step is really a series of smaller steps as you will break the walk into small segments, going farther from home in each segment. Now you're outside (which at one point may have felt like a nightmare to you). Let's start putting one foot in front of the other. Remember to stay relaxed, breathe, and focus on your breath or maybe on your feet as they hit the ground. Focus on anything but how you feel and what you're thinking. As you walk, you will feel the anxiety rise. You may immediately panic. This is expected. It's part of the process. Walk slowly, deliberately, and in a relaxed, mindful fashion for as many steps as it takes to get to a level of discomfort that you cannot tolerate any longer. Stop there. Maintain your relaxed, focused state regardless of those feelings and sensations—for 60

seconds. Then slowly return home. Unwind, get yourself together, and live your normal life for a while. No need to focus on the walk. Focus on whatever else you want to be doing. After some time, repeat what you just did. This time, stay in that discomfort spot for 90 seconds or 120 seconds if you can. The next time, stay for 150 seconds or 180 seconds. You get the idea. Walk to the place where you feel like you can't go any farther, then stay there for longer and longer time periods, using your tools to remain non-reactive to the anxiety and panic. At this stage, even though each new rung on the fear ladder brings renewed fear, anxiety, and even panic, you will likely find that you are getting better at not reacting. You may find that you are still getting very uncomfortable, but that you are less afraid of how it feels, or that the fear subsides faster than it used to on the lower rungs of the ladder. This is progress! You're still not walking around the block, but you're closer to it than you were, and you're learning the skills of non-reaction. You're eliminating the old avoidance and retreat behaviors. You're slowly breaking that mistaken link between fear and danger. You're doing it! When you can get to this first "fear point" consistently and comfortably, It's time to move to the next rung on the ladder.

5. We could just extend rung number four all the way to that walk around the block, but I want to illustrate the process as clearly as I can, so let's use a new rung—walking farther. Once you've gotten past that first stopping point on your walk, It's time to find the next stopping point. This might be another 100 meters down the road, maybe to the point where you can no longer see your house. It doesn't matter where it is along the walking path. Your next point is where you feel the rising anxiety or panic is intolerable, and you want to run home. Don't. You know what to do. Stay there for 60 seconds, remaining as non-reactive as you can, then return home to relax and regroup before repeating this as often and for however long you need to. You will find that your need to repeat and extend at each step in the ladder will decrease. Just be patient and accept

how the process works. Reset and repeat, then move forward to the next "stopping point" and do it there. too. You must understand that it doesn't matter how long this takes. It may be days and days. That is fine. You are learning with each outing. It all matters, and it all adds up!

At this point, you've been working the process and going up the fear ladder rung by rung. You're being patient, persistent, and tenacious. You're building your walk around the block bit by bit. It is hard work. Sometimes you are discouraged and want to quit. Sometimes it seems like you will never be normal again if It's talking you this long to walk around the block. None of that matters. Keep taking steps up the ladder in the systematic way I'm showing you. It's going to work.

One day, you will find that there is no more stopping point. You will walk entirely around your block. When that day or hour comes, you will know that you're not going to stop because you don't have to. You will see that you're going to complete your walk.

You will be elated. I am experiencing feelings of joy and getting a bit emotional writing about it. I remember how it feels. I can't wait for you to feel it, too. You will see your house getting closer with each step. Not because you are retreating and aborting, but because you have completed the task you set out to achieve. You may feel a rush of emotions. You may want to scream in victory or burst into tears. You may simply pick your chin up and confidently walk back into your house, knowing that everything is now possible where once nothing seemed possible.

Congratulations. You can cross that walk around the block off your calendar and off your goals list. You did it. You did what you once thought you couldn't do. Be proud. Celebrate. And by celebrate, I mean to do it again as soon as you possibly can. Right away, if practical. Take that walk again and again as often as you can for the next day or two. Own it. Love it. Make sure your brain knows without a doubt that you are safe, in control, and totally OK on that walk.

These are victory laps.

Relish them. You've earned them.

As a bonus, you're also consolidating your new skills and knowledge in your brain. This is part of the learning process. Repetition, once you've reached a goal, cements new information in place and makes you better at what you've learned to do.

Now, using a walk around the block as my example means there are some things I need to clarify quickly. You may genuinely have to build up to a walk around the block, and it may, in fact, take you days or even weeks to get there. That description may be quite literal for you. Conversely, where I describe days, you may only need hours.

In some cases, you may only need minutes between repetitions. Some goals you will reach by climbing your fear ladder in two hours. Others may take days or longer. There is no absolutely correct timeline and time scale. It will vary based on your current state/level, and the particular goals you're working on.

Now, it's time to take all the things you learned by building your walk around the block and apply them to the next item on your goals list. The same process applies. You will break that item into small chunks on a "fear ladder." You will work on each piece, moving up the ladder toward your goal in a repetitive, systematic, incremental way. You will continue to work on being non-reactive when the expected anxiety and panic arrive. You will begin to get comfortable with the process. It won't be a mystery. You'll know what to expect, and you'll learn that you can handle it when things get a bit bumpy. Do you remember when I said that achieving your early goals will help you more rapidly achieve your later goals? You'll see that in action as you attack each item on your list in the way I'm teaching you to do it.

I want you to take note of a few essential takeaways before we move forward. These are the concepts you should grasp at this point:

Never run. As you can see, I was very careful to tell you to stay in that anxiety/panic situation for an increasing amount of time at each rung of the ladder. NEVER run when you panic. Always stay and work on staying for more extended periods. Retreating to the safe zone when anxiety and panic hit teaches your brain the wrong lesson. This isn't about getting to a "place" then immediately running back to safety. This about getting to a "state," then staying in it before exiting. *Read this paragraph 100 times if you need to before moving on. It's that important.*

Expect to feel bad.

This process works because you are intentionally doing things that make you afraid and anxious. *It doesn't matter how you feel. It matters what you do.*

Expect that with each rung up the fear ladder, anxiety and panic will return. This is going to happen, so be OK with it. You're going travel a path that will take you from valleys of discomfort and fear, over mountains of comfort and calm, then back down into the valleys. That's how it works.

The good news is that over a long enough time, you will see that the valleys are not as deep, and the mountains are not as tall. The landscape will begin to even out. You are not doomed to ride the roller coaster of death forever. The process will get easier over time.

In the next lesson, I want to refine the concepts of being systematic and incremental and tie them back into the ideas of being consistent, patient, and tenacious. When you're ready, Let's do it!

Lesson 4.5

The Overall Plan.

The Method. The System.

Being Incremental.

We've now resolved to take action, set your goals, and talked about how to break them into small bits that you can tackle in sequence.

You've learned the concept of the fear ladder and how to use it to reach each goal incrementally. I've been throwing a ton of information your way, so now, let's consolidate it and wrap up with some essential concepts.

Executing your recovery plan involves being systematic, methodical, planned, and incremental. This isn't a random process. You're not going to work it by the seat of your pants. You're not going to make it up as you go along, and you will NEVER set your plans for a day based on how you feel when you wake up that day. You will plan and schedule your exposures and other exercises (i.e., meditation, breathing, muscle relaxation). Unless there are practical scheduling deterrents that pop up or an actual illness, you will keep your exposure appointments with yourself.

Think of this as a job you've accepted. When you accept a job, you become accountable to a boss. In this case, the boss is YOU. You must be accountable to you, which means making a plan and keeping to it to as high of a degree as you possibly can. Yes, there will be adjustments as discussed, but those are adjustments based on progress evaluation, NEVER on how you feel or being afraid. Your recovery plan and its execution should be a priority in your life. Do not relegate it to being an afterthought. You are worth the attention, effort, and time. Don't short-change yourself or set yourself up for failure by going "halfway" into this endeavor. Assign a value to your recovery, and don't let that slip.

BE METHODICAL

Being methodical means understanding that you will be following a process and trusting that process. When you want to jump ahead four steps, stop.

Trust the process.

When you want to skimp on the ancillary exercises, don't. Trust the process.

When you want to give up because you feel like crap and it's been a stressful day, don't. Trust the process.

You are relying on a METHOD that has been proven for decades to be the most effective way to treat anxiety disorders, so use the method.

Don't forget, your anxiety isn't special, unique, different, or worse, so you don't have to adapt or modify the method or the process. The technique I'm teaching you here works.

Work it. Stick to it.

As part of being methodical, it's best if you decide what your primary sources of anxiety-related information and support will be now. Do not spend every waking moment listening to every anxiety podcast, watching every anxiety video, and chatting in every anxiety Facebook group. That is counterproductive.

Limit your anxiety-related social media intake. Choose sources that align with the method you've chosen to follow. Choose sources that educate, inspire, and encourage. Resist the urge to use social media as reassurance or soothing. You may experience this feeling at times, but do not allow being on social media to be a significant part of your day every day. Drowning yourself in six anxiety books, ten YouTube channels, six podcasts, and five Facebook groups is going to make being methodical difficult. Pare it down. Be selective.

BE SYSTEMATIC

Being systematic means, you will work inside a system that involves some basic parameters. Those parameters look something like this:

- Make your plan.
- Commit to it.
- Set your goals.
- Break them into small chunks.
- Tackle each piece one by one, then move to the next target.
- Periodically review and assess your progress. Adjust plans and goals as needed.
- Remain objective. Time your exposures whenever possible. Make your goals measurable. If you plan to say in that anxious/panic place for three minutes, there's no question as to if you did it or not.
- Expect to feel bad when moving deeper into fear. Do NOT allow yourself to judge yourself or your progress by how you feel. Judge based on how you *react* to

how you feel. Your development is measured by getting better at feeling uncomfortable without running or adding additional needless fear. Nothing else.

- NEVER run and retreat. NEVER. You are supposed to feel anxious and afraid when you go into fear. You are supposed to have fearful thoughts. NEVER run from them. Plan to stay put in that place/state for 60 seconds, 90 seconds, ten minutes, or whatever your plan includes. STAY THERE for that long. Then you can go back to your safe zone. This is CRITICAL.

- Remember that it's not about the place you arrive at, it's about the state you get into. Exposures aren't about place. They're about the state of being anxious, afraid, or even in a panic. If that happens in your front yard, then it's a valid exposure.

- Remember the three reactions that we're trying to change. The reaction before (anticipation), the reaction during your exposures, and the reaction after (the story you tell yourself).

- Take care of yourself physically. Eat well, do your best to not be sedentary. Sleep as best you can (I know this can be difficult). Don't obsess over what to eat —this isn't the cure for your anxiety—but give your body what it needs to function correctly.

PLAN AND SCHEDULE

Schedule your exposures. Schedule your meditation, breathing, and muscle relaxation practice. Put them on your calendar, including times of the day. When you commit to walking on Wednesday at 10 AM, there's no ambiguity or option to think about it all day or wait until you feel OK. You do it on Wednesday at 10 AM.

Be sure to include time every day to practice your meditation/focus skills, breathing technique, and muscle relaxation skills. This goes hand in hand with your exposures. These are the skills you will be using while doing your exposures, and they must be practiced. Ten minutes for meditation and five minutes each for breathing, and muscle relaxation will go a long way. More is better, but this is the minimum.

Commit to doing your ten minutes of meditation, your breathing practice, and your muscle relaxation practice upon waking, right after breakfast, after dinner, before bed, or at some other predetermined time so that you aren't tempted to skip these tasks. It doesn't matter what time you choose. Just choose a time and stick to it.

Yes, things will come up from time to time. That's life. If you suddenly have to bring your cat to the vet, or your sister gets a flat tire and asks for your help, don't freak out. Simply adjust your day around those little surprises and do the best you can. Tomorrow is another day. Remember, it's OK to also live life while you recover.

While we're on that topic, make time in your schedule for things other than recovery. Read a book. Listen to music. Talk to your partner. Paint. Cook meals you enjoy. Watch a movie. Go bowling. Exercise. You have to also *live*. You can't be recovering 24/7. That doesn't make progress go any faster, and it will get exhausting quickly. Do the work, then take your breaks. That's part of the method and the system here.

BE INCREMENTAL—AVOID THE ACCEPTABLE BUBBLE!

When you're getting good at some tasks, it can be tempting to just stick to those tasks and forget that you have to keep moving forward in increments. When you've made your way through a few items on your short-term goals list, you will have built a bit of an "acceptable bubble."

This is the bubble you wind up in when you can get through daily life again without having to rely on others to do the basics for you all the time. You can shop; you can do the school run; you can maybe even get to work or school if that was part of your short-term plan.

When you get into the "acceptable bubble," it can be tempting to take your foot off the gas and slow down or even stop. Do NOT do this. Keep going. Push forward toward your midrange and even long-term goals. Staying in an acceptable bubble is one of the most common reasons for "relapse." I encounter people on a far too regular basis who tell the story of "beating" anxiety only to have it suddenly and mysteriously return down the road. When confronted with some basic questions, these people almost invariably discover that they built themselves a small acceptable bubble, then lived in it.

They never entirely lost the fear of anxiety and panic but instead engineered enough comfort to get by. When the acceptable bubble is pierced by life in general, suddenly, they declare that anxiety and panic are back. The fact is they never really left. Anxiety and panic have simply been waiting outside the bubble.

Working incrementally and being tenacious about going all the way through your recovery plan is vital to making a full recovery. Do not allow yourself to get complacent thirty-five percent into this thing. It will come back to bite you one day. It almost always does. Commit to full recovery and keep moving forward with your goals list even when it seems that you've got it all figured out. Trust me on this one.

We've spent this chapter talking about DOING, being patient, setting your recovery plan goals, breaking them into small chunks, and the big picture of what your plan looks like and how you're going to execute it.

In the next chapter, we'll go into detail on what it means to execute your plan. We'll talk about prioritizing, getting your loved ones on board, how to judge and assess your progress, what to do when you struggle, what tools and skills you need to work on daily, and how to integrate your recovery plan into life in general.

We're getting to the home stretch now.

After the next chapter, if I've done this well, you'll have gone from confused, disheartened and lost, to educated, empowered with a plan, and ready to move confidently in a clear direction toward recovery.

This is getting exciting, so let's keep going!

CHAPTER 5

EXECUTING YOUR

RECOVERY PLAN

Lesson 5.1

Prioritize and Commit

It's time to start executing your recovery plan.

This is where the doing actually starts. The good news is that this is where recovery happens. The bad news is that this is also the hard part. This is the part that requires you to do things that you are terrified to do and have been avoiding for so long. Very few humans beings—maybe none—enjoy being afraid and uncomfortable. I'm not talking about adrenaline junkies who love bungee jumping and rollercoasters. That's a different kind of afraid. Very few would choose to intentionally put themselves into what they are convinced are life-threatening or sanity-threatening situations. It's not our natural state, nor is this intuitive in any way.

In this chapter, you are going to start ignoring your self-preservation instincts. You will surrender and do the opposite of what every cell your body is screaming at you to do.

Am I making you anxious?

Am I making you reluctant to move forward?

Do you really want to do these things?

Isn't there an easier way?

WHY isn't there any easier way???!!!!!

I'm not trying to freak you out. I'm trying to illustrate a point. When confronted with difficult, scary tasks, you will want to find a way out of them. This is natural. You will look for shortcuts and excuses, especially on the days where you are feeling it so strongly.

When you are convinced that you need to hide under your covers and shake, what you are trying to do gets even harder. Everyone on this journey encounters these feelings. It is normal and to be expected.

The secret is to find ways to combat the natural tendency to escape and avoid when your plan requires executing! The problem is that humans are creatures of comfort and prefer the path of least resistance. How can we expect and prepare for the inevitable—making excuses? How can we be ready to smash these excuses when they pop up?

The two tools I can give you here are prioritization and commitment.

PRIORITIZATION

You must make yourself and your recovery a priority in your life. To get things started, you have to put yourself at the very top of your list. Yes, this means you go to the top of the line even before your children, your partner, and your job. No, this is not selfish. I promise it's not. It's quite literally the opposite of selfish. Hear me out.

"Everyone is counting on me."

"I'm always the one getting things done."

"I have to hold it all together."

I've heard these statements and countless variations of them literally thousands of times. I do understand them. I had to go through the hardest parts of recovery while my daughters were quite young. I know that it is challenging to manage both the recovery process and your role as a parent. Our relationships with our significant others, friendships, family bonds, and our ability to make a living and feed ourselves all place daily demands on us.

Demands on our time and attention are quite real. They add difficulty to the task of executing a recovery plan. They can also become excuses. You will need to be brutally honest with yourself in this respect. Remain aware of when you are making excuses designed to avoid doing the work that needs to be done. When you are feeling bad, your confidence is low, and you don't want to do your exposure work or practice your breathing or meditation, you will be tempted to tell yourself that there's "too much going on" and that you don't have time to work on your recovery tasks. This is not helpful to you in any way.

Your family (for example) requires your attention, but right now, YOU need your attention more than they do. You may be tempted to play the "I'm being selfish" card at times when the going gets rough. Don't do this. While this might not be what you want to hear, I want you to consider which is really more selfish. Bringing your anxiety and fear into your family, relationships, and career for the rest of your life or taking some time for yourself to make sure that doesn't happen?

Spending time now to ensure that you are a better version of yourself later isn't selfish. It's smart, and it's actually the opposite of selfish. Intentionally doing difficult, scary things to change your life will benefit the people you love just like it will benefit you. The people close to you are also impacted by your anxiety problems. They see your struggle. They feel it emotionally, and practically, too. They want you to be better. So do you think they would see it as selfish if you took measures to get better?

In the end, "selfish" is just another distortion invented by your fear to perpetuate itself. Do not allow yourself to fall into this trap.

You're going to have to take a little time to sit with this and reflect. Are you ready to put yourself at the top of your priority list? Are you prepared to be totally honest with yourself when you're using "too busy" and "I'm being selfish" as excuses for not making time to do the hard work? Are you ready to invest time and hard work now to get the life you so desperately want later?

If you are prepared for all of these things, then before we get started, put yourself at the top of your priority list. Promise yourself that you will stay there at all costs, at least for a while. The time will come where your progress will allow you to integrate other obligations into your schedule without impacting your plan or recovery. You will be able to make your plan just another part of your life rather than your sole purpose in life. That will happen, but to get there, you have to make recovery your number one job.

COMMITMENT

The other tool you can use to avoid making excuses is commitment. Entire libraries full of self-help books are written about this topic. But, I do acknowledge, it's complicated. Commitment means deciding to work toward a goal, then doing that work even when you can think of 1000 reasons not to. Commitment is fluid and flexible, never rigid, but also never failing. Commitment teaches us lessons and builds skills. It builds strength of character. We admire commitment. We aspire to it. We are inspired by it, too.

Why then, is it such a hard thing for so many people to truly embrace and integrate commitment? I wish I could teach you how to get and remain committed to your recovery. But I don't think I can.

You may already be the type of person who makes a commitment and doesn't let go until a job is done. Congrats. You are ahead of the game. If this is you, you can likely skip forward a few paragraphs. But if you are not typically this type of person, you will need to find a way to show commitment to this process.

I can offer a few ways to view commitment that may help you find it.

- First, commitment isn't a mountain.

- Commitment equates to every step it takes to climb that mountain.

- Commitment isn't a significant life-altering choice.

- It's an unbroken string of much smaller "moment defining" choices.

- Commitment isn't something you are. It's something you do.

- Commitment doesn't require the absence of doubt.

- Commitment doesn't mean always being sure or confident in every moment.

- Commitment doesn't equal motivation.

- Commitment is momentary in nature but driven by a long-term view of your life and the world in general.

- Commitment has courage and discipline in its DNA.

When it comes to your recovery plan, commitment requires the acceptance of things that you do not like and would rather avoid. You must accept what is, to achieve what can be. Commitment in recovery means that you are trusting the plan you created and the concepts upon which it was built. If you don't buy it, you won't do it, so be sure that you understand why this is the best way out.

You don't have to like it, but you do have to adopt it as your new approach. You must be willing to build belief in the plan through action. And you will believe in the plan when you execute the plan. Commitment means being OK with the fact that you're not totally OK with the state of things and acknowledging that you won't ever be OK with them until you do it and learn.

Commitment to your recovery plan means looking at all the excuses, including the ones I just wrote about here and deciding upfront that you will dismiss them when they pop up. I encourage you to write all your excuses down and nail that list to your wall if it helps.

Here are some examples of excuses and the responses that will help you refute them:

- Excuse: "It's too hard." Reality: I CAN DO HARD THINGS.
- Excuse: "It's soooo scary." Reality: I CAN BE AFRAID AND SAFE AT THE SAME TIME.
- Excuse: "It feels like..." Reality: WHAT IT FEELS LIKE DOES NOT EQUAL WHAT IT IS.

- Excuse: "It's taking too long." Reality: MY BRAIN NEEDS TIME TO HAVE ALL THESE EXPERIENCES.

- Excuse: "I'm not strong enough." Reality: I'VE BEEN STRONG ENOUGH TO GET THROUGH PANIC AND FEAR ALL THIS TIME ALREADY!

- Excuse: "I have no time for this." Reality: HOW MUCH TIME HAVE I SPENT BEING LESS THAN I WANT TO BE BECAUSE OF THIS? I HAD TIME FOR THAT, DIDN'T I?

- Excuse: "Nothing works for me." Reality: I'VE BEEN DOING THINGS THAT WERE NEVER GOING TO WORK. THAT DOESN'T MEAN THAT NOTHING EVER WILL.

I can easily keep going with this list.

You can, too.

You can help yourself stay committed to your recovery plan by listing all the excuses you can think of for why you should stay in bed rather than dragging yourself through discomfort and fear. Then, respond to your excuses appropriately while calm and rational. Refer to those responses when tired and feeling overwhelmed and afraid. They can help you remain committed.

Another tool that can help you stay committed to your recovery plan is a promise to never judge your progress based on how you feel. Progress is judged based on what you do. Remember, you want to assess facts, not feelings. Your plan told you to drive to the supermarket and sit in the parking lot for five minutes. Did you do it or not? How you felt while you did it isn't the point. Do not allow the subjective, overly negative aspect of how you felt to erode your commitment to this plan. You are going to feel bad, especially at first. But you are learning to feel bad with a positive outcome so that you can learn to not be afraid of feeling bad. Do not lose sight of that. Remain focused on the objective of building the commitment your plan needs.

In the end, commitment means making a choice to do what needs to be done, sometimes on an hourly basis.

And commitment matters most when you're just starting out, and what you are undertaking will be most challenging. It will matter most when you hit those rough patches that make you want to throw in the towel and try something else. In a difficult moment, deciding to make the right choice rather than the easy choice, is what demonstrates and cements commitment.

The good news is, you don't have to be 100% committed to the grand concept of a new life. You merely have to be committed to each decision and choice you have to make to enable you to live your new life. Break it down, use the guiding principles I've pointed out above, and commit to your plan one choice and decision at a time.

I promise that as you go down this path, executing your plan moment by moment even when you don't want to, momentum will build. Choices will get easier to make. Strength and courage will grow. You will begin to achieve what you want to achieve. Then the desire to continue achieving will start to outweigh the desire to avoid fear and discomfort.

If you've spent any time in my Facebook group (https://theanxioustruth.com/links), you've likely seen people look forward to challenges and describe them as opportunities to get even better. This is what commitment breeds over time.

Commit to the plan and its execution, and you can be one of those people, too, even if that seems entirely unbelievable right now.

Now that I've spent two thousand words or so sounding dangerously like some kind of cookie-cutter cringe-worthy motivational life coach, let's recap and look forward to the next lesson.

Before you start to execute your plan, be aware that you are about to do challenging and scary things repeatedly. This will no doubt make you look for excuses to not do them. We can set ourselves up to succeed by expecting this to happen, by being prepared, and by using the concepts of prioritization and commitment to squash potential excuses before they become roadblocks.

In the next lesson, we'll talk about how to arrange your life to support your recovery plan. There are practical things you can do from a scheduling and logistics perspective that will give you the best chance of succeeding. We'll take some time to go over a few of them to get you started on the right foot.

Lesson 5.2

Arrange Your Life Accordingly

We've spent the last lesson going over prioritization and commitment to your recovery plan.

Now, let's take some time to talk about arranging your life to accommodate the work you need to get done. You can make your recovery a priority, and fully commit to the plan, but you may have to shuffle some things a bit to make room for all this. The best of intentions won't matter if your days are such that you have zero actual time or the space to execute your plan. We need to look at ways to make additional time in a busy schedule. We're also going to have to be honest about the amount of time you currently spend doing easy but non-productive things each day.

NO BREAKS. NO DAYS OFF.

We've already seen that this work must be done daily, or even several times each day. A recovery plan can quickly lose its effectiveness if you're doing the work sporadically when you *kinda* think you can fit it in.

Working on exposures and other practice only on the weekends, or with long breaks between events, isn't going to get you the results you're hoping for and need. To get the ball rolling, recovery has to become at least a part-time job for you. For some, it becomes damn near full time. One of the most common mistakes I see people make is to approach their recovery inconsistently.

They might engage in a few days of hard work, then a few days of none. They might have a day of working on active recovery, followed by two days on the sofa or hanging out in a safe zone.

When you approach your recovery plan this way, you are shortchanging yourself. You are going to wind up frustrated and discouraged when progress is slow or hard to come by.

That means you are going to have to do this work every single day with no days off. This is going to require that you make room in your daily routine, schedule the work, and stick to that appointment. While that might sound like a drag or a needless level of "hardcore recovery-ness," remember that we must always guard against the natural tendencies of humans to seek comfort. If you do not arrange your life to accommodate your recovery plan, you are inviting failure. If you leave things to chance and random puffs of motivation, you will almost inevitably fall into the comfort trap.

Comfort and ease feel good.

Intentionally doing hard things does not.

Which do you think you will choose if you're making it up as you go along without a schedule to follow? You know the answer and so do I. And you also know that choice won't help you.

THE MORNING EFFECT

Many years of interacting with many anxiety sufferers have allowed me to see patterns. One of the most apparent patterns is what I like to call the "morning effect." The morning effect is what you get when you start your day in motion—actively engaged with your recovery plan. When the first thing you do each day is work on making forward progress, you will find that you are in a noticeably better place come afternoon and evening. Using the morning to your advantage serves a few purposes:

1. It keeps your exposure and practice from becoming a dreaded task shrouded in anticipatory anxiety. Waking up at 6 AM knowing that you have to take a problematic walk or drive at 4 PM is adding more

difficulty than you need to have. Starting the day with the difficult tasks takes away all the anticipation and dread.

2. It sets a tone for the rest of the day. Accomplishing something to start your day puts you in a way better frame of mind than lying in bed, just thinking about how you feel. It doesn't matter how small the accomplishment is. It will always be better than spending your first hour of the day ruminating, thinking, and dreading what is to come.

3. It adds structure. Having a purpose when you open your eyes matters. Having a pre-defined plan to execute matters even more. Often a person in the grips of anxiety and panic is confused, unsure of him or herself, and has difficulty making decisions and choices. An unstructured day that starts with a totally blank slate often adds to anxiety and fear when the anxious person can't think of what they should do next to feel better. Building structure into your day starting with a pre-defined morning routine

means you don't have to make it up as you go along every morning while afraid and unsure.

Given the "morning effect," the first thing you'll want to do is arrange to give yourself an hour or so immediately upon opening your eyes to work on what you have to do. Open your eyes, get your feet on the floor, and at a minimum, get yourself ready for the day. A trip to the bathroom. A glass of water or a cup of coffee or tea. Brushing your teeth. Combing your hair. Getting dressed. This is a morning routine that you don't have to think about. You can just do it, regardless of how you are feeling. This routine takes lying in bed thinking, ruminating and dreading, and replaces it with motion, purpose, and small tasks completed. It's an accomplishment. Use it to your advantage.

If you can immediately move from your morning routine into exposure work or practicing your new skills (breathing, muscle relaxation, and basic meditation), then do that. If you're working on walking around your neighborhood, you can do that once dressed in the morning. The same goes for driving. There really is no need to put off doing what you can do in the morning. It's true that some things just can't be worked on at 7 AM, but wherever possible and practical, use that first hour of your day to practice the needed skills and do the required exposure tasks. If you have to get the kids off to school, then either get up early enough to practice your recovery before you have to tend to them or go through your routine to get ready and dressed, get the kids taken care of, then immediately move onto your recovery tasks for the day. If you have to go to work or school, then get up a bit earlier and do what you can before you have to leave. If you are in a panic every morning while driving to work, then use some time before work to be in the car to practice that.

I'd also add that when you do the heavy lifting to start your day, you will feel satisfaction at the end of the day. Knowing that you accomplished something and have "earned" the right to be tired and take a rest, can go a very long way. You'll likely find yourself a bit more motivated and less susceptible to negative judgment about your progress. If you have a less than desirable afternoon, you will be able to counter that with the knowledge that you were moving forward before things went south on you. You'll be able to look forward to the next morning as another chance to get things back on track.

The point here is that you will want to rearrange your morning schedule so that you can get as much of your recovery work in as possible to start your day. Trust me, it will matter.

SPRINKLE IT IN

You will also want to carve out some time throughout the day to practice your new skills. You don't have to do exposures all day long, but you will get better at relaxing and refocusing—which are both SO crucial along the way—If you practice more often. Practice in the morning, but also schedule some time to practice essential meditation/focus, belly breathing, and progressive muscle relaxation for 10-15 minutes a few other times throughout the day. Remember that your goal with these activities is not to instantly make yourself feel better. You are learning new skills that you will use as you execute your recovery plan. You'll need practice, and you won't be very good at these things in the early days. But as with any new skill, more practice is...well...better!

I know your life may be busy, with plenty to do every day, but remember what I stressed about commitment and prioritization. I need to make time! Build-in another few 15-minute blocks to practice in the afternoon and evening, too. Five minutes of breathing, five minutes of progressive muscle relaxation, and five minutes of meditation/focus practice isn't all that much, and it will matter going forward.

MONITOR YOUR DOWNTIME

The last tip I can give you about rearranging your life to support your recovery efforts is to make use of time when you have it. Schedule things as I have detailed in this lesson, but also do not be afraid to seize the opportunity to use your free time to make progress. When you find yourself with a break in the day, take another walk, or another drive. Do some more work on whatever recovery goal you are currently addressing. This may involve breaking some bad habits. You may default to staring at your phone, reading anxiety forums, or watching YouTube or Netflix when you have downtime. *As a rule, if you have no demands on your time during the morning and afternoon, use it to your advantage!*

And not to worry, your guilty pleasures and hobbies will still be there in the evening.

We all need time to relax and indulge in what we enjoy, so don't feel guilty about doing these things (or whatever else you enjoy doing). Just do them AFTER you've done your scheduled recovery work and taken advantage of any surprise free time that pops up. This is another one of those recommendations that can really help you avoid that negative spiral where you judge yourself harshly and feel that you are never going to get better. When you use your time to do the work rather than defaulting to more comfortable activities, it means when you do get to do the fun, comfortable pastimes, they are more meaningful.

Earn your free time.

You'll feel better about yourself and your overall recovery progress when you do.

Admittedly, I am not a terribly rigid person. My days are rarely fully scheduled, if at all. I am guilty of making things up as I go along. This is my natural tendency, and in general, it works for me. During recovery, however, that all had to change. I had to become brutal and relentless in the way I structured my days to ensure that I did all the work that needed to be done. I did not like running my life that way, but I knew it was required if I was going to get where I wanted to be. So if you find what I am saying here to be a bit over the top, or if you can't see any need to be scheduled and structured, take it from the voice of experience.

This really is the best way, at least until you build a fair amount of momentum, and you're well past the beginner stage. I hate a schedule as much as any human walking the planet, but in the context of solving my anxiety disorder problem, I embraced the need to schedule, and I am better off for having done so. I think you will be too.

Before moving on to the next lesson, take some time to think about your schedule. Does every day look the same? Do you have regular days off from work? What about your family and kids? How does their schedule fit into yours? Think about where you will make the changes I've talked about and how you can accomplish those changes. Then, take some quiet time and reflect honestly on the amount of "slush" time you have in your days. Most of us have more than we're willing to admit. If all this scheduling and planning seems difficult, maybe just exchange an hour of scrolling through Facebook and Instagram for an hour of active recovery.

In the next lesson, we'll talk about ways to involve your family, friends, and those close to you in your recovery plan.

Lesson 5.3

Get Your Family And Friends In Line

Like it or not, most of us have family and/or close friends who are impacted by our anxiety issues. They watch us struggle. They may try to help in whatever way they think is appropriate. They sometimes grow frustrated and impatient with us. They have the benefit of seeing us through eyes not clouded by irrational fear. Most times, the people close to us just want us to get better, to feel better, and to rejoin them in living life. They have opinions and ideas that sometimes help, and other times cause friction. We lean on them for support and comfort when things are difficult. Our friends and family members are with us on this journey and will continue to be as the journey turns toward recovery and life reclaimed.

This can be both a blessing and a curse.

Friends and family members can be a great source of support and encouragement. Unfortunately, they can also be negative influences, sometimes inadvertently. Even the best of intentions can go awry in the absence of a clear understanding of this problem and the path to a solution. Given that the ultimate responsibility for our recovery lies with us alone, it is essential to strike a balance between having support when you need it and having "too many cooks in the kitchen."

Before your recovery plan starts to unfold, it can be an excellent idea to get your family and friends on board with your plan. Let me be clear from the start. You are responsible for making your plan and executing it. You are responsible for understanding the principles upon which your plan is built and for staying close to those principles. You are not trying to get your loved ones on board to help you carry the burden, to guide you, soothe your fear, or make you feel better. You want your friends and family to act as cheerleaders, motivators, and rational eyes at the times where your vision may be clouded by fear, fatigue, or discouragement. This is what I mean when I say you'll want them on board with your plan.

So how should you address this?

What should you tell the people closest to you about what you are about to do? How much do they need to know?

What are you going to ask them to do?

What are you going to ask them NOT to do?

The answers to these questions can vary depending on personal preferences and life circumstances. Let's set forth some general guidelines that you can use to inform your family members and friends and to set them up as allies who will act in the best interests of your success.

There are different ways to get your family on-board with your recovery plan. Some people may choose to gather everyone together and "officially" address their intentions in a grand gesture. Some will speak to friends and family members individually. You may want many people to be aware of what's going on, or you may want to limit those in the know to a select few. You may wish to share tales of your work regularly, or you may choose to execute your plan in relative silence. There is no right or wrong way when it comes to these issues. There are a few basic rules, however, that will help you get the most out of your personal support circle. Let's go through them.

1. Everyone needs to know from the start that you are not asking for opinions or judgments on the soundness of your plan or the approach you are about to take. Some family members and friends will disapprove of what you are doing based on what they "know" about anxiety. Most times, they mean well. They don't want to see you struggle and may not fully understand why you are choosing to intentionally be uncomfortable. In some cases, they will default to projecting their desire for comfort and safety onto you. This is natural and to be expected. Do not be angry or upset with them. They may not understand, nor do they have to understand for you to succeed. Explain that you have chosen this path based on a wealth of actual real-world data and the many people who have benefited from this approach. Acknowledge that it is difficult and that it may look strange to them when you are intentionally doing hard things regularly. Just ask them to take a leap of faith with you and cheer for you without judging the merits of the plan. I had to tell my family there was a "method to my madness." And I was

quite firm in saying that I was not going to solicit or entertain suggestions on what to do differently. You may have to do the same. For those members of your support circle that are interested in learning what you are doing and why, feel free to share this book with them. Have them listen to a few of my podcast episodes that directly address family and friends. This may help them to better understand what you are embarking on. Your family and friends people can be your biggest cheerleaders, and they will really appreciate what you're doing (since it benefits them, too), once they understand.

2. Ask family and friends for their support with scheduling and logistics. Your recovery plan requires prioritization, commitment, and often some juggling of routines and schedules. These will likely impact those closest to you, so you are going to have to ask them to help out with that. Be willing to bend now and then when there are scheduling conflicts, but in general, ask that they allow you to do what you need to do for the next 4-6 weeks to start. Your plan will

be evolving and adjusting over time, so you can always revisit the nuts and bolts of routines and schedules at regular intervals to keep everyone working together.

3. Explain to family and friends you do not want them to try to soothe or reassure you. This can be a major change for some of the people in your life. They may naturally want to do this. In many cases, you may have "trained" them to respond to your anxiety in this way. You must be clear with them when you explain that trying to reassure you that you are OK and trying to make you feel better with words is actually counter-productive now. Tell them that what you need to hear is: "We know this is really hard and uncomfortable, but you have to experience it to learn that you are OK." Explain that what you can't hear any longer is, "It's OK. It's only your anxiety. The doctor said you are fine. Come sit with me until you feel better." Explain to them the difference in these methodologies and why reassurance won't work to help you. Tell them you

appreciate that they care about you but be firm in asking that they abandon reassurance and soothing responses, even when your judgment is clouded, and you revert to old habits of seeking those responses.

4. Tell your family and friends that you need motivation and encouragement, not accommodation. Reminding you that the best time to do the hard work is when you feel bad is VERY helpful. Validating avoidance or excuses for retreat is not helpful at all. Your support circle can help you remain committed to your plan by helping to get you moving when you'd rather hide under the covers.

5. If you prefer to work in silence and aren't inclined to share much, ask your family and friends to respect that. Explain that you will reach out when you need to, but that you would prefer they not ask you about the work you are doing unless you bring it up. If, instead, you are prone to sharing every detail, ask them to help you keep this to a reasonable level. It's not helpful to talk about this problem 24/7. The

words you use when discussing it matter. Remind them to remind you that talking about how you feel all the time is reassurance-seeking and counter-productive. Ask them to be firm with you on ensuring these behaviors are curbed (although they don't have to be rude or disrespectful). A gentle but firm reminder from your partner (for example) that he or she will not engage in symptom checking and scanning with you is what you need to curb your desire to verbalize it all the time.

6. Help family and friends to understand that you may or may not want to celebrate milestones and victories with them. Explain that when you do want to celebrate, you may be celebrating something that they consider no big deal. Acknowledge that the things you will be doing truly are no big deal, and that part of this process is just undoing bad brain habits that have caused you to forget this. When you celebrate, you are celebrating a lesson learned and a habit broken, not an actual drive around the block. It will help them to hear what you are actually

celebrating so they won't inadvertently minimize your accomplishments. Again, you are not required to share and/or celebrate but having this little chat will be helpful for if or when you do.

7. Ask for your family's and friend's patience. Explain that while we can learn a fear almost instantly, un-learning that same fear takes time and a systematic, incremental approach. Sometimes when people see you doing what you haven't done in a long while, they may get excited and push you to go faster. They may ask you to bite off larger chunks than your plan calls for. While your progress may, in fact, lead YOU to voluntarily and willingly change your plan and start to go faster, that isn't required, and it may not happen. People are going to have to be happy with your accomplishments and progress as it all unfolds with no particular deadlines. This can be difficult at times. I found that fully accepting responsibility for my role in the problem, and continuously putting in the hard work, made it easier for the people around me to be patient. They saw me owning it and putting

in the work every day. That mattered. Ask for patience from your family and friends but earn it, too. That's a win for everyone.

In the ideal world, the people in your inner circle hear you, fully support you and understand what you're doing, and either get out of your way or jump on the bandwagon to cheer you on every day. This may happen, but you may also run into conflict. This is natural. We're all human. We get frustrated, upset, and even resentful at times. Starting with these general guidelines and keeping the lines of communications open can help minimize the drama and the angst that pops up here and there.

Now, let's talk for a moment about belief and credibility.

If you've been struggling and living a limited life for a very long time, your loved ones may have seen you proclaim that you are going to fix what's wrong many times. They may have a limited ability to believe what you say or even to believe in your ability to pull this off. If this is your fifth plan in the last 18 months, you may have a bit of a credibility problem with your friends and family. While this isn't a feel-good issue, I'd be remiss in my duties if I did not address it. You may be tempted to be angry or upset with them if you get an eye roll or dismissive response now and then. When you are told, "We've heard this before," it can be hurtful. I get that. but we must accept reality.

If this is your reality, then you have to own it and use it as a tool to help you get and stay motivated and committed. You may have to SHOW your loved ones that you're doing it before they start to come around. Words alone may not be enough in the beginning. This is OK. Do not let it discourage or dissuade you. In all honesty, they might have a hard time believing your words when you start this new journey. You may have to show yourself that you can do it, too.

While It's not pleasant to confront a history of starts and stops, it can be a blessing in disguise. It can force us to focus on action rather than words, and as we have seen, this is a DOING solution, not a saying solution.

Now, I need to take a moment to address another unpleasant situation that I see far too often.

Sometimes recovery from an anxiety disorder exposes cracks in a relationship. I see this most often in instances where a person has been wholly dependent on his or her partner for an extended period. When this changes, sometimes the partner reacts unexpectedly. Newly developed strength and independence isn't met with enthusiasm, but with anger and resistance. Sometimes the partner feels they are losing the power and control they've come to enjoy. If, as you see improvement, you are surprised to note your partner is angry, aggressive, or trying to hinder your progress or otherwise keep you "under wraps," this is a red flag.

You may have to be honest with yourself about the nature of your relationship. Far too often, I see even long-term relationships exposed as controlling or even abusive in nature. Do not turn a blind eye to this or make excuses for the bad behavior of a partner. If you are unfortunate enough to find yourself in this kind of situation, carefully and quietly reach out to people you can trust to help you assess or even exit the situation. If need be, seek professional assistance. Recovering from an anxiety disorder is stressful enough. You will be working hard to get your life back. Do not allow someone else to take that from you.

In the next lesson, I'll explain how to fill your toolbox with useful goodies to use while executing your plan. But before going on, take some time to think about how you want to inform and involve your family and close friends.

Think about what the ideal situation would be from your point of view. Consider the issues that may be important to them. Try to formulate a "friends and family plan" that will work for everyone. It will be time well spent.

Lesson 5.4

Sharpening Your Skills

Back in lesson 3.6, we went over the three vital skills you need to develop as part of your recovery strategy. These skills are not magic anxiety killers or panic shields, but they will be essential as you implement your recovery plan. A regular practice designed to develop and sharpen these skills should be incorporated into your plan.

To refresh your memory, the three vital recovery skills we need are:

Physical relaxation on demand: Learning to find tension in your body and learning how to release that tension to achieve a state of physical relaxation and limpness. Getting good at relaxing your body on demand is the first skill you need to change your reaction to anxiety, panic, and fear.

Proper breathing: Breathing into your belly, using your diaphragm rather than your chest and shoulders. Slowing your breath and allowing your exhales to be slightly longer than your inhales. The skill of slow, gentle diaphragmatic breathing helps us avoid over-breathing (hyperventilation) and the disturbing sensations that come along with it. Breathing correctly also helps us slow things down, which is a much better response to fear and panic than the usual rushing around and speeding up.

Focusing selectively: The skill of selective focus is likely the most critical skill for you to develop and master. Through the practice of basic meditation skills, you can learn to focus where you want to focus—on demand—rather than on where your irrational fear and anxiety want you to focus. The ability to focus on something other than the sensations in your body and the thoughts in your head is essential in the act of surrender to these scary sensations and thoughts.

One of the most common errors I see people make when implementing and executing a recovery plan is forgetting to make time to practice these new skills. There is often much discussion of relaxation, breathing and focus methods, and how to do them. There's also usually an acknowledgment of how vital these things are. But in many cases, there is no attempt to actually engage in practicing these skills every day. Without regular practice and repetition, there is no improvement in your ability to relax, breathe properly, and selectively focus. No mastery of these tools is achieved.

In this scenario, the anxious person that is not practicing basic meditation skills every day (for example) will continue to ask for help with the surrender and "do nothing" process. They will argue that it is difficult and that they can't seem to get the hang of it.

The anxious person that is not practicing relaxation, breath, and focus regularly will often assert that they are just not able to do these things, or that they simply don't work. This is no different than buying a guitar, only picking it up when you want to play a song, never practicing, then wondering why you can't actually play that song like an expert guitarist.

The heart of your recovery plan is experiencing fear without reaction. Your exposures are the fear experiences. Using these three vital skills is the non-reaction part. They must go hand in hand. Exposure without being proficient in non-reactivity is frustrating. It's not terribly predictable in its outcomes, and it leads to disappointment and discouragement. Being an expert non-reactor is excellent, but unless you use that alongside movement toward your fear, that skill alone won't really help you solve your anxiety problem. We need BOTH. Exposure and proficiency in being non-reactive. When in the process of actively facing and going toward your fear and anxiety, you will use these tools and skills actively. They will facilitate the experiential learning your brain needs to back out of the corner it's in. In a nutshell, you're going to have to get better at these things to get the best results.

Let's talk about how you get better at these things so that you can use them as the essential tools they are for you.

To start, you must actually DO these things.

You must practice relaxing your body.

You must practice proper breathing.

You must practice basic meditation (selective focus training). Not for hours on end, but at least a few times every day for a few minutes here and there.

You are not required to sit and meditate for three hours. You are, however, required to learn how to do it. The step I need you to take right now is to embrace this idea, even though practicing these skills might make you anxious. You must get OK with the notion that these are things that will help you, and that you will have to put in some time and effort to learn them and build basic proficiency.

Before we get into suggestions for exercises and a practice schedule for each of these three tools, let me address the single biggest objection I see to doing what I'm talking about. Whenever I suggest to someone that they learn to relax, breathe, and silently focus on their breath, there is a chance that they will tell me that they've tried it and that it doesn't work for them. I hear the same responses again and again:

"I'm just not into meditation."

"I tried all that, but my brain won't turn off. It doesn't work."

"When I sit quietly and try all that, it feels terrible. My anxiety gets even worse."

"I want to do things to get better, but there's no way that my anxiety will let me sit that way quietly. I have to be on the move or doing something to keep my mind occupied."

Do any of these things sound familiar to you? Have you ever said them to yourself? If you have, don't worry. You're in the company of a vast number of people who resist this approach and declare it too scary, impossible, or out of reach.

Many times I encounter people who listen and agree, but then come back weeks or months later with the same problems and the same questions. For some reason, they're just not "getting" recovery, and they are frustrated and discouraged. In many of those cases, when pressed, these people will admit that they either rarely practice these new skills or have never even tried them once.

If you want to learn to play the guitar and your teacher asks you to practice every day, you're going to have to practice. If you refuse for whatever reason, it would be odd to ask the teacher why you're not improving.

So if you are feeling resistance to the idea that you must learn to relax, breathe, and focus as part of your recovery plan, take some time to think about this. Yes, these things may be scary and uncomfortable at first. You will likely be bad at them when you start out. All of this is to be expected. Everyone felt that way at first! But just like you must be willing to make some genuinely awful noises the first time you play that guitar, you must be willing to struggle a bit with these new skills, too.

Do not expect that you will sit and instantly turn your brain off or knock down your anxiety. That will simply not happen. It will take time and repetition to improve your ability to do the "surrender things" when anxiety and panic are in full swing. This is OK. I promise this is a good use of your time.

I've mentioned several times that when you're working on your recovery plan, you will need to include some time to practice your skills. This isn't just about running out the door to walk, drive, stay home alone, or whatever it is you have been afraid to do for so long. You must work on your skills, too. A baseball player learns to hit, throw, and field the ball while also playing in practice games and actual competitive games. Baseball teams don't just show up for the games. They practice, which includes working on the basic skills required to play the sport. You will do this, too. You will do your exposures and meet your challenges, but you will also take time to master the skills required to "do recovery." Let's go through them one at a time so we can talk about exactly how to practice these things.

RELAXATION

Learning to relax your body might sound pretty basic and straightforward, but when you are in an anxiety state and full of fear, you may find it difficult or near impossible to "just relax." Meaning you can learn a relaxation routine, practice it, then follow it when you need to reverse the tensing and bracing your body has created in response to anxiety and panic. This routine is called progressive muscle relaxation. It's taught all over the world for a good reason. It's a simple routine, easy to understand, and very useful. When you practice progressive muscle relaxation, you familiarize yourself with the sensations of tension, and also with the sensation and feeling of relaxation. It teaches you to recognize when you are tense and what to aim for when releasing that tension.

You will intentionally tense, then relax, the muscles in your body. This is done in sequence, usually starting at your head and working your way down to your toes. There are some really excellent progressive muscle relaxation tutorials on the internet. You can use the basic free tutorial on my website to learn and practice with at https://theanxioustruth.com/skills. Go ahead and start there if you'd like. My progressive muscle relaxation tutorial only takes a few minutes to go through. I also have links to other excellent relaxation lessons and tutorials that I can recommend.

BREATHING

This is another thing that might seem odd. How could it be that a human being needs to learn how to breathe? That's a fair question.

When I talk about proper breathing, I'm merely talking about learning to slow your breathing and to breathe in a rhythm that keeps you from accidentally fueling your anxiety and fear. When afraid and anxious, most people will naturally breathe harder, hold their breath, or engage in an unending series of huge breaths and heavy sighs. These are all attempts to calm down. Often people engage in a combination of all of these breathing patterns. They do not help. They can make things worse, putting you into high gear or even causing those scary tingling/numb feelings and tunnel vision associated with hyperventilation.

When we learn to breathe correctly, we are merely learning to slow the breath, breathe into the belly without moving the chest or shoulders, and to exhale for longer than we inhale. Three basic ideas make this an easy plan to follow, but many people do find that they need to practice this often to break some bad breathing habits. I have a free diaphragmatic breathing tutorial on my website at

337

https://theanxioustruth.com/skills. I also link to other proper breathing lessons and tutorials that you may find helpful.

Finally, focus and mediation. This is the big one. It's also the scariest one for many because it's the activity that puts you face to face with all those scary thoughts and sensations without resistance. This is the surrender tool. The goal here is not to learn to reach some higher spiritual plane but to simply learn how to place your focus selectively where you want it and to return to that selective focus point when distracted.

That's all it is.

Basic mediation and focus skills merely teach you how to let your body and brain do what they are doing while you focus elsewhere without resistance. Mediation is learning the art of non-reactivity. I find that the best way to learn this skill if you are new to it is to use an app like Calm, Headspace, or Insight Timer. All three are very well-reviewed online, and all three have free versions that can be very helpful.

I am going to suggest that you try one or more of these apps as your introduction to basic meditation. You can find a free tutorial on my website: https://theanxioustruth.com/skills. You are welcome to use this whenever you would like to, but you will find that you'll want a bit more instruction than I can practically offer. Start with my tutorial, then give Calm, Headspace, or Insight Timer a try to see which one works best for you. Trust me on this, even if you struggle at the start with meditation and selective focus, you will be happy that you took the time and made an effort to learn it.

Let's take a moment to touch on the idea of using guided meditations that include music, nature sounds, and continuous verbal instruction during meditation. These are quite popular and can be found easily on YouTube. Guided meditation is a great relaxation tool. It's not a great focus tool. Some people prefer to start with guided meditations because they feel that it's "easier." I won't go so far as to tell you not to do this, but I do want to point out a common mistake. Many people opt for guided meditations because they are simply afraid of being alone with their thoughts. Using music, sound, or a human voice to "drown out" the thoughts you fear isn't really going to help in the long run. Use guided meditation as an introduction if you want but accept that at some point sooner rather than later, you have to actually learn to sit quietly with your thoughts and practice re-focusing away and maintaining a state of calm non-reaction. That is the whole point, and in my opinion, guided meditation isn't really going to teach you to do that.

I suggest that as part of your recovery plan, you schedule time at least twice every day to spend a few minutes each on muscle relaxation, breathing, and basic mediation. A total of 10-15 minutes spent practicing these things in the morning, then again in the evening, would really great. At least to start, practice these three things as individual skills twice per day. Over time, you will see that you won't have to practice muscle relaxation and breathing directly. They will just become a natural part of your meditation practice. It all starts to flow together over time as you get better at all of it. But to start, work on all three of these skills one by one every single day. It will matter.

I will acknowledge that for some of you, just practicing these skills twice (or more) every day will be like exposure. You may spend some time primarily working on these three items without too much else going on. That's OK. If you need to build a little foundation with relaxation, breathing, and focus before you start executing the meat and potatoes of your exposure and fear ladder plan, this is perfectly acceptable. Just be careful not to confuse learning to relax your muscles with recovery. They are not the same thing.

Sometimes people get caught up in a groove where they are just meditating and breathing all day long without doing the other work. While they may get very good at breathing and focusing, this is not recovery. This leads to a realization over time that these cool new skills haven't done anything by themselves to improve the overall anxiety disorder situation. Give yourself a few days or a week to work on these three items, then sit down and really be honest about moving on to the actual work.

In the next lesson, we'll talk about the difficulties and struggles you will encounter while executing your recovery plan. These are to be expected, so knowing what's coming and being OK with it can really help.

Lesson 5.5

Expect To Struggle

This is a lesson that I wish I didn't have to write, but I'd be leaving out an important bit of information and experience if I didn't write it. Before you read on, I am going to remind you that I did everything that I have written about up to this point.

I lived this thing.

I was you.

And I'm still here, better than ever.

Millions of others have also traveled this path before you. They also encountered obstacles and challenges, yet still completed the journey. Do not get discouraged, and do not let any of this frighten you. It is better to be prepared with a detailed and realistic road map. I could paint you a rosy picture to make you feel better or inspire you, but that would be the easy way out. Inspiration is great. It's not everything.

Expect to struggle as you execute your recovery plan. It happened to me. It happens to everyone. It is to be expected. Unfortunately, this is not an easy process. There will be struggles, uncertainties, and periods of slow progress. Trust me on this. It will all be worth it.

Don't misunderstand me. You are not going to live in a torture chamber for the next few months. Nobody is going to beat you with a stick as part of this process. You won't be shot at, stabbed, or called names, but you will still struggle, nonetheless. The struggle is in learning to ignore your body and mind when it literally hits the panic button. The struggle is in telling your self-preservation instinct to sit down and shut up. The struggle is in doing hard, scary things, again and again, to learn that they're not actually hard or scary. The struggle in this process is primarily mental and emotional. It isn't about enduring pain. It is about enduring doubt, uncertainty, and disbelief.

Recovery from an anxiety disorder does not happen along a straight line either. Progress toward freedom from anxiety, panic, and fear is like the stock market. From hour to hour and day to day, stock prices rise and fall. Money is made and lost. This is normal and expected. One rarely succeeds or fails in the market based on two trades made on a Tuesday. One succeeds by having a smart investment strategy executed over time. A smart investment strategy rarely involves huge trades that make you millions overnight. The most successful people invest wisely in proven companies. They go with what has been shown to work. Most importantly, they are patient and willing to play a "long game."

This strategy also applies to your recovery plan and it's execution. You are not day trading with anxiety and fear. You are playing the "buy and hold" long game with it. You are building a plan based on what works, knowing that it takes some time to complete that plan. It is very important to remain aware of this as you go about the business of getting your life back. Do not expect every hour to be better than the previous hour. Do not expect every day to include giant victories and steps forward. As jazzed as you may be about kicking anxiety in the rear end, this is not an express elevator to the top of the recovery mountain.

It is a common experience for people to struggle more when first starting out on this new path. This is normal. You are learning how to do new things and how to approach your anxiety in a totally different way. The struggles thus tend to be many in the early days. The good news is that when you stick with it, it gets better. In later days you will be more advanced in your recovery. The struggles will then be fewer but can be harder from a mental and emotional standpoint. When you've gone a long way, it can be hard to feel like you've been dragged back to the starting line (even though that doesn't actually happen.) This is also normal and to be expected. You will struggle more in the early days. You will struggle less later on, but those struggles may be deeper. Keep this in mind as you go.

Now let's talk about the different struggles and challenges you will likely face along the way.

Some days you will not want to get out of bed to face the hard work. You will be tired. You will be sick of being afraid and on edge and unsteady. Frustration will set in. You will get angry with yourself. Sometimes you will get angry with others in your life because they are not doing what you "need" them to do. You will sit and wish it all away, knowing that it doesn't work that way. You may find yourself full of regret, sadness, or anger over what you see as so much time wasted on anxiety and fear. You will be tempted to beat yourself up over how this problem has diminished the person you used to be. You will think of yourself as a bad parent, partner, friend, or employee because of anxiety. Some even experience a crisis of faith or spirituality during recovery. They may wonder if a higher power has abandoned them or is punishing them. These are the emotional and mental obstacles that you will face as you execute your plan. Expect them. Do your best to prepare yourself for these obstacles and recognize them when they pop up.

When doing the actual work itself, you will hit roadblocks. You will try to meditate and focus for five minutes while your mind is racing at close to the speed of light. You will attempt to relax your body, and your body will put up a fight. You will want to do the work but will find yourself almost paralyzed with fear that tells you that you can't. You will want to allow fear to wash over you, but your survival instinct will scream that you must do something to save yourself. The weather will change on you, introducing new road or travel conditions. This may cause you to incorrectly gauge your safety again. This will fuel more fear. You may get sick with a cold, a stomach virus, or some other ailment. Your fear of your own body will turn a simple temporary condition into what you may be tempted to call a "nightmare." Schedules will get disrupted. Family and friends will accidentally make things difficult for you sometimes. On some days, maintaining some semblance of a life will feel like a huge burden added to an already full plate. These are the practical challenges and obstacles that will struggle along the way. Again, expect them and prepare for them.

It helps to have a plan in place that you can refer to when it comes to struggle and challenge. When you feel like you're stuck in cement, progress is coming at a slow pace, and you think you can't do this, what will you do? I would suggest saving this lesson somewhere convenient so that you can see it regularly. You'll need a reminder that the struggle you're experiencing is part of making progress. This lesson is that reminder. Use it. I would also suggest talking about this and sharing this lesson with someone close to you. When you struggle, it is helpful to revisit information like this to gain perspective. It can be more helpful to have a person (or people) point out that you are sitting passively in the struggle rather than taking action to address it.

Online support groups can be a useful part of your "struggle contingency" as well. Use them as a source of motivation and inspiration (not only for sympathy and soothing). Whichever way you choose to execute it, having a plan is always going to be better than feeling defeated and directionless.

Look at the differences in the thought processes and how one will move you forward on your path to recovery.

"I'm struggling and lost. This is a hard place to be."

"I'm struggling. So, I will go back and re-read, learn, and look for sources of encouragement and motivation to get me past all this. This is still hard, but it's way better than the first option."

Do you see the difference?

I want you to remember that anxiety disorders are masters of deception. Anxiety, fear, and panic are excellent at magnifying and distorting EVERYTHING bad. They are also excellent at hiding and minimizing everything good. A bad day quickly turns into hours of lament and fear that you will never get better. Panic during an exposure that had become easy for you can be turned into an exasperated feeling that you are back to square one. The realization that your progress hasn't been fast enough to get you to some important event may get warped into a three-day catastrophe in your head. Remember this at all times. Write it down on your wall if you have to.

ANXIETY AND FEAR ARE LIARS AND MANIPULATORS!

Do not forget that there WILL be struggles and challenges. It can help to remember that they will not actually be as disastrous as your mind will make them out to be.

I know that challenges and struggles can be demoralizing and discouraging. I'd like to share some of my own personal experiences with you in the hopes that it will provide you with a little inspiration to keep going. I want you to know that I lived what you are living now. I was you. I went through all the ups and downs of recovery. You will not find a more determined, driven person than me, but I struggled, too. I promise I know what it feels like.

I will admit that I never doubted my ability to get better. That may simply be part of my personality. But even in the face of a high sense of confidence and competence, some days were discouraging. Actually, some days were VERY discouraging. Many people hear me speak, or see me on video, and conclude that I'm "super strong." They assume that it must have been easier for me than it is for them. Untrue. There were moments when I wanted to go to sleep for a very long time to get a break and forget about this job I had to do. There were days when I was shaking, unsteady on my feet, and my heart was pounding like a jackhammer. I had to literally drag myself out the door to do the work. For a while, my energy levels varied between tired and exhausted. I was very frustrated on days where I felt like my progress was too slow. At times I was plain angry at the whole situation and at me for having gotten myself into it.

Especially in the early days, my recovery wasn't fun in any way. It felt like a very large mountain to be forced to climb. I did not breeze through this process by any stretch of the imagination. While I was very consistent in my approach, that doesn't mean that everything went forward at a fast pace every day. I assure you, it did not, even for me. I struggled. I faced mental, emotional, and practical challenges that were difficult to go over or around.

As time went on, as it will for you, I saw hours here and there that showed real promise. Those hours then became days. Not consistent days. One good day, then three less than ideal days that felt like crap. Then there would be two good days in a row. At some point, the struggle became less a part of the journey. My brain was learning new lessons and un-learning the bad lessons it needed to leave behind. The fear wasn't constant and pervasive. The anxiety habit was breaking over time. The clouds started to lift. Then there would be a day that felt like it came straight out of the first week of my recovery. I would get SO angry and impatient and frustrated by that. Invariably, that would pass, and the skies would turn blue again for me. It was quite a rollercoaster of ups and downs.

In retrospect, I can say with absolute certainty that my recovery—like the stock market over a long enough time—was always trending in a positive direction. Even when it didn't seem like it, progress was being made. But in retrospect, I could not recognize this progress until later on. It was progress, however. I know now that even the "bad" times served a teaching purpose. They provided experiences that became part of who I am now. The lessons that I learned through the struggle still serve me well today and will for the rest of my life.

You will struggle.

I struggled.

We all struggle.

I promise you that you will not struggle forever. Knowledge, planning, determination, and the experience and guidance of those who have come before you will get you through. You will find blue skies after the storm. I know you will.

In the next lesson, we'll talk about avoiding the judgment trap and how best to judge and evaluate your progress during recovery.

Join me.

Lesson 5.6

Judging Progress Properly

I'm going to give this to you straight.

Again.

How you feel doesn't matter.

Without going back to re-read the previous 60,000 words, I'm reasonably sure I've said that before. But it really does need to be said again here in this context.

As you are executing your recovery plan, you should never judge success or failure based on *how you feel*. The change you seek is not in how you feel. The change you are attempting to enact *is in your reaction to how you feel*. In recovery, feeling anxious or afraid is never a failure. It does not represent a step backward. Not ever. Let me explain.

No human being lives a life free of anxiety or fear. Attempting to banish anxiety, fear, and uncertainty from your life is a futile mission. It can never succeed. Recall that an anxiety disorder isn't about being afraid. *An anxiety disorder is about being afraid of being afraid*. The disorder is about reacting to how you feel with fear, avoidance, and escape. Remember that anxiety and fear are not keeping you stuck. Being afraid of the anxiety and fear is what has you in the position you are in. This being the case, we are working to drop the disorder, not the anxiety underneath it. Stop being afraid of how you feel, and you have won this war. What now seems paralyzing and insurmountable becomes a relatively minor obstacle.

We are working toward eliminating the disorder. The disorder is based on a fear and avoidance reaction. What, then, is your goal? Is your goal to not feel a certain way? Is your goal to not experience certain sensations? Are you trying to not think certain thoughts? Or, is your recovery goal to change your reaction to these things? I think you know the answer now.

Your goal in recovery is to change your reaction to anxiety and its accompanying physical and mental states. This is what teaches us that we no longer have to fear it all.

If this is your goal, then should you be measuring success, failure, and progress based on how you feel? Of course not. You only measure your success and progress in recovery based on *what you did*. The yardstick is not your state. The yardstick is your reaction to that state. When you are doing those hard, scary things that you have to do as part of your plan, you will feel the things you hate to feel. That's not what you care about. You only care about your reaction to feeling those things. Let's look at a typical example to see where things go off the rails for most people.

Here is a very common post that we see almost daily in my Facebook group:

"I've been doing so well for the last week. Almost no anxiety at all! But today I woke up with raging anxiety. It's been really hard to even get myself out of bed and out the door. I feel like I'm back at square one."

Can you see the error here? This person is making a judgment based on how they feel. They feel anxious and afraid, so they declare failure and a slide back to the beginning of the road. This statement is driven (understandably) by emotion and fear. It's rife with the catastrophic distortion. Anxiety disorders are so good at creating this. Invariably, when someone posts this message, they will be met by responses that encourage objectivity. They will be asked to look at what they are DOING, rather than how they are FEELING. Did you get out of bed? Did you get out the door? Are you working on relaxing and refocusing while you do these things? Then you are moving forward! When our frustrated friend (the poster) changes the angle of attack, most times they wind up in a much better place. With a simple mindset shift, a day that started "so badly" ends fairly well. A potentially lost opportunity to learn is shown for what it really is. Progress.

This is why we do not judge our success or failure on how we feel. We never measure our forward progress based on emotion and fear. How you feel does not matter. What you did matters.

I do need to clarify a bit here. People sometimes take my words to the extreme. We are not learning to be robots here. We are learning to not be afraid of our own humanity.

If you are ill, then of course how you feel matters. If, for example, you end a relationship, lose a job, or experience the loss of a loved one, then how you feel matters. When in recovery, it is perfectly acceptable to feel ill or emotionally upset. You are human and allowed to experience what life throws at us. When this happens, you are not required to ignore it all and press on like some kind of soulless cyborg. Instead, you must experience whatever emotion comes out of that particular situation. In this case, your recovery focus needs to temporarily shift toward eliminating needless additional fear. In other words, feel what you feel based on the situation but work on not being afraid of feeling it. When things begin to settle, as they always do, and the life event passes for the most part, then you can shift your focus back to executing your plan.

It is natural to get swept away by emotions sometimes. Remaining objective at all times about anxiety and recovery is quite difficult. When fear, anger, and frustration set in, judgment tends to get clouded. This is normal for all humans across many stressful and difficult situations. I've written about the role of friends and family in this process. I've alluded to the use of tools like online support groups. As you begin to execute your plan, consider what you will do when you get into this state. If you fall into the trap of judging your recovery based on how you feel, how will you recognize that? Who can you rely on to point out what you are doing? Is there anyone that you can count on to help you shake it off and get back into a more productive frame of mind? This is where willingness to seek motivation is much more important than the desire to seek reassurance or comfort. When things get sticky for you, it might be nice to hear 15 people in a Facebook group tell you that "it's OK." It is more constructive and productive, however, to turn to people who will help you adjust your course. It might not feel quite so warm and fuzzy to hear that advice, but warm and fuzzy is not going to get you out of this situation.

I'd like to take the opportunity here to revisit another related item. Building as much objectivity as you can into your actual activities and exposures is vital. If you are planning to meditate/focus for three minutes, you have succeeded if you do the three minutes, even if it was hard. If your plan for the morning was to walk around the block, or make a few phone calls that make you anxious, how you felt while doing those things isn't what you care about. Be sure to make your activities as measurable as you can.

"I will walk around the block twice."

"I will drive to the mall and sit in the parking lot for five minutes."

"I will call the dentist and the hairstylist to set appointments."

See how measurable these things are? You either walked around twice, sat for five minutes, or made two calls, or you did not. If you did not, then do it again. It's quite simple.

There is no judgment clouded by being afraid, shaking, being nauseous, or hating what you have to do. You did it, or you did not do it. When we measure our success and failure that way, it goes a very long way toward keeping you moving forward.

Not everything in life is measurable, quantifiable, and able to be timed. When engaging in life events (as opposed to planned exposures), it is not practical to declare that you will stay at a birthday party for exactly 18 minutes. In those cases, you may not be able to measure. You must still do your best to maintain focus on what you are doing rather than how you are feeling. Did you go to the party? Did you continually react with relaxation and refocus when fear washed over you? If you can answer those questions with a "yes," then you've won. Pat yourself on the back, even if you felt like you were going to lose your mind or get violently ill a few times during the event. You still made progress. Recognize it. Don't let anxiety and fear take that away from you.

It's not about how you feel. It's always about how you react to how you feel.

In the next lesson, we'll address a topic that is confusing to many. *What is recovery, and what is life? Can they both happen at the same time?* Take a few minutes to shake off all your old attachments to how you feel, then turn the page.

Lesson 5.7

It's Not Always Recovery

Recovery happens. But life also happens.

It's going to be essential to integrate the two. They exist side-by-side. More accurately, they are entwined with each other. You can't put your recovery in a box all by itself. If life is a soup, then recovery is an ingredient in that soup. You can't take the salt out of the soup once it's in there. In the same way, the process of recovering from an anxiety disorder cannot be segregated from the rest of your life. While actively executing your recovery plan, you are still making "life soup." Let's look at ways to make sure it tastes good when It's finished.

You cannot actively recover 24 hours a day. That's not practical or even possible. In the beginning, many people become consumed with the process of overcoming the disorder. They read, research, talk, and discuss. They become obsessed with knowing everything possible about this thing they are doing. They often spend time examining every thought, action, and situation within the context of the recovery process. The questions can be endless for some:

Should I be doing this now?

Am I supposed to be having these thoughts?

Did anyone else do (insert thing here) during recovery?

Am I doing it right? What about now? Am I doing it right now?

This can lead to a blizzard level white-out in a person's brain. Zero visibility and hazardous road conditions. It can sometimes create a bit of paralysis. Attempting to categorize and judge every moment of life within the context of anxiety recovery can lead to getting stuck. It's a particularly nasty kind of stuck, too. The kind of stuck where you really want to do move forward, and you're willing and ready to move forward, but you're just not. Let's look at how to stop this from happening.

First, you are going to have to accept that life is happening all around you at all times. You are living life right now. Life isn't a thing you're preparing to do after your recovery is complete. You've been doing life since you were born. You've had no say in the matter. This will not change. Accept that recovery is just another life project. That planned exposure to the supermarket is recovery, but it is also life. Make an effort to get your brain around this idea. Learn to take a few moments to appreciate the fact that life is happening.

Next, Let's look at the reciprocal relationship. Recovery is life, but life is also recovery! You will be tempted to over-analyze everything that isn't specifically part of your recovery plan. You may worry that accepting an invitation to share a cup of coffee with a neighbor isn't "right." Your child's upcoming holiday band concert could become a source of stress for you as you try to make it "fit" into the context of your anxiety disorder. I am asked all the time about vacations, family functions, job interviews, parties, picnics, and a wide array of other typical life events.

The questions are always the same.

"Should I do that? If I don't, is that avoidance? Am I doing too much? I don't want to trigger a setback!"

The answers will vary according to where you are in your plan. If you are just starting out after being housebound for five months, trying to "push through" a long weekend in the mountains with your partner might not be the best idea. The fear ladder is part of your plan for a reason, and it should be respected, especially in the early stages of recovery.

As you advance, however, these events and situations will become part of your recovery process and progress. Attending the company picnic may represent a challenge. If that challenge matches the level you're at on your fear ladder, then do it. When you do it, try to remember that you're not going to the picnic only because you need to make progress. You are going to the picnic because you are working on learning how to live your life again. Not everything must be judged in the context of anxiety. Sometimes sharing a hamburger with a co-worker is just sharing a burger with a co-worker. It's important to remember this and to do your best to appreciate that aspect of it as well.

We know that not everything in recovery is black and white. Not everything is obvious to us in a given moment. Not everything can be accurately and objectively measured. Relaying the concepts in this lesson is difficult because the integration of recovery and life is a moving target. The connection is always there, but how you view it changes as you progress. When your relationship with anxiety and fear begins to change, you will find yourself more receptive to the idea of simply living your life at times. At first, recovery is recovery. As time goes on, while you are doing the work, recovery becomes life and life becomes recovery. I urge you to remain open to this concept as it begins to reveal itself to you.

I'd like to take a moment to address the idea of "breaking the rules." This comes up often. A wedding may be an event that a recovering person wants to attend, but there may be a concern that going outside what is viewed as recovery will be too much. Often I see the mistaken belief that there are special recovery rules that forbid certain activities. Remember that recovery is not only about learning how to experience anxiety and fear healthily, but it is also about rebuilding a healthy relationship with life in general.

When we remove the misguided fear that drives the disorder, we must re-acclimate to life without constraints and constant worry. A wedding might be outside the letter of your recovery plan, but it represents a chance to experience a regular life event in a new way. As you progress, the "rules" of recovery relax and even blur. Do not be afraid to incorporate life into your plan spontaneously. Remember that when you do, feeling bad is not an indicator that you made a mistake. Keep your life-centric goals in mind, resist the urge to declare failure based on feelings, and tell yourself a success story. Being at a wedding is living life, even if you had to excuse yourself a few times to let panic pass. Recognize that you lived life—albeit uncomfortably—for a few hours. Compare that to the days when you vehemently refused to engage in similar activities. Pat yourself on the back for the accomplishment. Remain open to those opportunities as they present themselves.

Life will not present itself only as significant events like weddings and vacations. Life is opening the mail. Life is taking a shower. Life is raking leaves in your yard. Life is reading a book about the Roman Empire because you are a history buff. Life is blowing your nose and getting dizzy for a few seconds because your ears are plugged. Everything is life. Just do it all, even when you are feeling anxious and afraid. Take the opportunity to appreciate that even the act of brushing your hair can be an exercise in slowing down, being mindful, and quieting your anxious brain. Live the small moments of life, doing your best to apply the principles of recovery as you go about your day.

Now, let's talk a bit about the idea of "overdoing it." This is a concern I hear all the time about life events. When stepping outside the bounds of your recovery plan to join friends for dinner (for example), you may feel anxious while there. You may feel anxious afterward, or even the day after. This is not because you "overdid it."

I have seen far too many people declare that they must stick to walking around the block and meditating because they felt bad after taking an impromptu trip to the movies. They fail to recognize that they actually did some living. They fail to acknowledge that what they did represents a change and a challenge. When we are learning to not fear anxiety, we will feel anxious. When we are learning how to live life again, even when uncomfortable, we will feel uncomfortable. The fear and discomfort experienced after an unplanned trip to the park with your children are no different from the fear and discomfort you experience after a planned exposure. Life is no more dangerous than what you may have narrowly defined as recovery.

Recovery is life.

Life is recovery.

Within the context of incremental challenges and a systematic march forward into recovery, life is never "overdoing it." Embrace all the challenges and remember that the discomfort is required as part of your progress.

Finally, I want to touch on the drive to have someone confirm and validate every life choice you make along the road to recovery. This is not required. At first, you are learning. You will have questions and will be unsure of things. Guidance from people who came before you can be helpful. As time goes on, however, you must learn to trust yourself. Start considering that you should default to "yes" when it comes to life. You do not have to ask your therapist, partner, or online support group if it is OK to go to the movies or attend a concert. Be careful about asking for someone else's approval of your life choices as they relate to recovery. We're all unsure at times, but in those uncertain moments, we must learn to make our own choices and trust that we are capable of dealing with whatever happens as a result. This includes meeting that cute guy or girl for coffee when they ask. Maybe you will feel amazing the whole time. Perhaps you will be anxious during and panic afterward.

Either way, there is a lesson to be learned, and you will be able to handle every outcome. Your friends cannot teach you how to live again. This is something you must discover yourself through experience.

I will close this lesson by re-stating that life and recovery are joined at the hip. While everyone loves the idea of recovery, life sometimes gets a bad reputation in anxiety circles. This is not fair. Life is good. Allow yourself the opportunity to learn this again.

Next up, let's take a look ahead at what comes in later stages of recovery, and what you have to look forward to at the end of your anxiety journey.

Spoiler alert...It's amazing.

CHAPTER 6

WHAT'S NEXT?

When you started reading, back in Chapter 1, you were likely anxious, afraid, confused, and lost. If I have done my job well, you should now have a better understanding of where you are.

You should understand how you arrived in this lousy place through no fault of your own. You now have knowledge that you didn't have, and a point of view that maybe you had never considered. Above all, I am hopeful that you have some measure of new confidence in the direction you must take. I hope that you believe in the plan you must execute. You were afraid, anxious, confused, and lost. My wish is that you are now educated, empowered, encouraged, and motivated. I want you to see more than just hope now. I want you to see both a plan and the promise of a better life. Most importantly, I want you to know that YOU have the power to build that life.

So, what comes next? What can you expect as you execute your recovery plan? Is it really possible to live free from fear? What will your new life look like?

What comes next is plenty of hard but immensely rewarding work. Ups, downs, highs, and lows. There will be moments of defeat and despair, but also moments of victory and happiness. The path from fear to freedom is long and winding, but full of experiences that will teach you lessons.

There will be lessons in patience and persistence. You will learn new ways to view the world. Things that seem like threats to you now will be easy to dismiss when you are done. You will build confidence and discover your inner competence. Nobody goes through this process without gaining an appreciation for how strong and able they really are. The hard days will teach you compassion for yourself, which in turn will teach you compassion for others. You may be praying for the return of the "old you." But you won't get the old you. You will get an improved version of you.

This problem, and the process of solving it, can feel like walking through fire. It may be, but there is gold forged in those fires. One day you will look back and be grateful for what you learned from all this.

BUT...

Is it possible to really recover?

Is a life free of irrational and misplaced fear possible?

Is recovery just a pipe dream?

These are questions that I hear every day. I understand why they are asked. When you are struggling, and it seems that every day is a failure, it can be challenging to see the light at the end of the tunnel. Let me say this. I have invested thousands of hours in this thing over many years because full recovery is one hundred percent possible. I lived it. I have made friends along the way who have lived it. My Facebook group, and especially my team of brilliant admins and moderators, is full of beautiful people who are fully recovered. They give their time to help guide those still on the journey. I didn't invent any of this, nor am I making it all up. Millions of people in the last 50 years have fully recovered using the approach I am advocating here. It's not new in any way.

This is not just a dream. No matter what habits and patterns you are trapped in today, it can all change. It is not easy or comfortable, but it is very possible. I would not have spent the time that I have on this book, another book, a podcast and a community of thousands of human beings if it were not possible.

So, what will life look like after recovery?

Without all that misplaced fear, there is no avoidance. There is no need to retreat or escape. There are no safety rituals or special requirements for you to get through a day. You won't get through days. You will *live* them.

In a post-fear life, you will experience human emotions without being afraid of them. After recovery, you will find yourself able to plan, and set a course for yourself, without being obsessed or paralyzed by worry. Your sense of internal direction will grow. This is the ability to make choices and trust yourself without endless doubt and questioning. Your craving for external guidance and validation will fall away. Knowing that you are capable of doing life on any terms, you will act more confidently and assuredly than you ever imagined possible.

Life after recovery will include challenges.

These will be challenges of growth, achievement, and satisfaction. You will no longer be challenged to simply exist and survive. Your ability to accurately and objectively assess challenges and threats will surprise you. Life will seem easier. Less will ruffle you or bother you. When you have lost your fear of anxiety, you will no longer lock yourself in a protracted inner debate over attending a family reunion, taking a new job, or moving to a new apartment. Removing irrational fear is a fantastic thing to do for yourself. It makes you a better leader, a better parent, a better partner, and a better human being in general.

This is why I say that you will find the old you along the way, then you will keep going forward into a new you. Everything great about you before this anxiety problem surfaced is still there. You will rediscover it, then enhance it. This experience will not only teach you lessons, but it will also make you a better learner going forward. A world with fewer perceived threats is a world full of greater possibilities. You will find yourself open to new ideas and new directions. You will be comfortable challenging your own world views and ideas because you will know that you are more than just your thoughts, beliefs, and fears.

I realize that I am painting a very rosy picture here. I'm not trying to sound like the stereotypical motivational speaker. I am simply relaying the facts as I know them. It just so happens that this particular set of facts is dripping with awesomeness. After writing over 70,000 words about how hard this is, I thought I owed you a glimpse as to why this journey is well worth taking. As I write this, I use the word "you" in the spirit of speaking to a friend. I have been able to meet many real people along this path I have chosen, and one day I hope that I will be able to meet you too in some way. Maybe we are already friends, or at least social media acquaintances. Perhaps I have never heard your name or seen your face. Either way, I am genuinely excited by the thought of what lies ahead for you.

My experience with many humans has been that it's not really fear that holds them back. It's a belief in themselves. Many people stay stuck because they do not believe they are capable of facing fear. Some don't think they're worthy of recovery and a better life. Others don't believe it possible because they have been taught that life is nothing but a series of disappointments and failures.

If I could give you one gift, it would not be courage. It would be belief. I want more than anything else to provide you with faith in yourself. From belief flows courage, determination, and the desire to make your world and the world around you a better place.

Maybe you don't believe in yourself right now. That's OK. I believe in you. Just borrow my belief until you find yours. You don't even have to give it back. Just pass it along to the next person who needs it.

A better life awaits. Now go get it.

Acknowledgments

Dr. Claire Weekes, author of *Hope and Help For Your Nerves*. Dr. Weekes was an Australian physician that wrote what I consider to be the gold standard when it comes to explaining the basic principles of the approach I take with anxiety and anxiety disorders. Everything I've ever said or written on this topic has its origin in her work. *Hope and Help* taught me what this problem is, and generally how to solve it. If there was no Dr. Weekes, there would be no "Anxious Truth."

Laurie Yorke, my dear friend and steward of the PaxilProgress website. While PaxilProgress no longer exists, Laurie taught me how to create a community that truly helps human beings in distress. If you've ever benefitted from being in my Facebook group, or from anything I've ever presented on the internet, you can thank Laurie for teaching me how to help you.

"JP of Diamonds." I don't know JP's real name, or where he is today. JP had a YouTube channel back in 2008 or so, on which he shared openly his story of panic disorder and recovery. When I was struggling, I watched every second of every video on JP's channel. The channel no longer exists, but it was JP that planted the early seeds of my podcast in my mind. Watching him talk about this issue inspired me to do the same.

Billy Cross (Anxiety United). Emma. Sarah. Ben. Sabrina. Natalie. Chrissy. Chris. Seth. Sharon. I'm sure I'm missing a few people here, for which I apologize. These were the friends I made on YouTube when I first started making anxiety and recovery videos back in 2008 or so. We would post exposure videos for each other, encourage each other, inspire each other, and generally help each other. That little group morphed into a social network named PanicStation that Billy and I ran together for a couple of years. We had a few hundred members at one point. The entire social media community surrounding my podcast is a direct descendant of PanicStation. I owe this fine group of humans a debt of gratitude that I will never be able to repay. When I was doing the hard work of recovery day in and day out, they were along for the ride. I'm thankful to count several of them among my friends even to this day.

The community surrounding my podcast is something I value highly. I consider it a privilege to be able to interact with so many people on a daily basis, all of whom are just looking for a better life. Watching them learn, grow, progress, and in turn help others, is one of the most rewarding experiences I've ever had. This community could not exist without the help of an amazing team of people that I call friends. These are the admins and moderators that help me keep things focused and on-message all the time. They are what make my community different than any other anxiety-related social media community you are likely to find anywhere. So I extend my deepest thanks and admiration to Holly, Ingvild, Diane, Connie, Alexis, Babs, Dani, Joyce, Andrew, Heather, Martine, Nick, Loui, and Jay. I could not do what I do without them.

I also have to extend thanks to friends who have helped me in the writing process. These fine people have read along with me as I've written, providing feedback and support. The contribution they've made has been invaluable. Thank you to Bethany, Rebecca, Monique, Donna, Wendy, Marsha, Julie, Lydia, Missy, Jessica, Mike, Keir, Amanda, Jaime, Judi, Nichole, Christy, Lindsey, Audrey, and Sorana.

About the Author

Drew is the creator and host of *The Anxious Truth*, a stunningly popular anxiety podcast that's been in full swing since 2015. With over 500,000 downloads (and growing), *The Anxious Truth* enjoys a large, vibrant, and engaged social media community of amazing humans supporting, inspiring, encouraging, and empowering each other to overcome anxiety and fear. Listen to a few episodes of the podcast, and you'll know right away that this isn't what you're used to hearing about anxiety.

Drew's unique, no-nonsense approach to solving the anxiety problem combines his strong, confident voice with genuine care, compassion, and a desire to see others learn and succeed.

You can find Drew, his podcast, and his community at https://theanxioustruth.com.

Having been through not one, not two, but THREE different periods of debilitating anxiety, panic, agoraphobia, and depression, Drew turned it all around in 2008.

Armed with a deep understanding of the cognitive nature of this problem, courage, and an intense desire to solve the problem once and for all, Drew rid himself of the irrational fear that fuels the disorder.

Now living a normal, happy, productive life without avoidance and retreat, Drew spends a fair amount of his time tending to his podcast, writing about anxiety disorder issues, and interacting with the large community surrounding his work.

A technology entrepreneur by day, Drew's true passion is using his own knowledge and life experience to teach and empower others as they work to solve their own anxiety and fear problems.

When he's not podcasting, writing, or taking care of business, you can find Drew attempting to be a proficient guitarist or in the gym. A fan of scientific inquiry, Stoicism, Taoism, and Buddhism, Drew is also a lifelong night owl who's probably staying up too late right now.

Oh, and Drew realizes that writing about himself in the third person is a bit ridiculous, but that seems to be the way it's done in these parts, and there's nothing wrong with a bit of ridiculousness now and then!

Disclaimer

I am not a doctor. I am not a licensed therapist or counselor. This book is simply the story of how I overcame my anxiety-related problems. It was written to provide information, inspiration, understanding, and hope to the reader. I have made every effort to ensure that the information in this book was correct at press time. While this book is designed to provide accurate information in regard to the subject matter covered, I assume no responsibility for errors, inaccuracies, omissions, or any other inconsistencies herein and hereby disclaim any liability to any party for any loss, damage, or disruption caused by errors or omissions, whether such errors or omissions result from negligence, accident, or any other cause. This book is not meant as a substitute for a direct expert in the advice of medicine or mental health. If such assistance is required, the services of competent professionals should always be sought.